THE SUCCESSFUL
INTROVERT

DR. REGINALD L. RAMSEY, PHD, MBA, CISA

authorHOUSE®

AuthorHouse™
1663 Liberty Drive
Bloomington, IN 47403
www.authorhouse.com
Phone: 833-262-8899

Published by AuthorHouse 03/20/2023

ISBN: 979-8-8230-0415-2 (sc)
ISBN: 979-8-8230-0414-5 (hc)
ISBN: 979-8-8230-0413-8 (e)

Library of Congress Control Number: 2023905231

Print information available on the last page.

This book is printed on acid-free paper.

Date: march 20, 2021, 3/23/2021, 4/10/2021; 11/13/2021; April 30, 2022; 5/7/2022; 5/16/2022; 5/19/2022; 5/21/2022; 5/28/2022; 5/29/2022; 5/30/2022; 6/12/2022; 6/14/2022; 6/19/2022; 6/26/2022; 7/1/2022; 7/2/2022; 7/5/2022; 7/7/2022; 7/17/2022; 7/23/2022; 7/24/2022; 8/14/2022 ; 8/16/2022; 8/17/2022; 8/26/2022; 8/28/2022; 9/3/2022; 9/4/2022

This book is due by April 30, 2023 … (12 months)

The working title for this book is "successful introverts."

CONTENTS

Definitions ix

Dedications and Thanks.. xi

Interesting Quotes xiii

Chapter 1 Introduction 1

Chapter 2 Leader Traits 9

Chapter 3 Hyper Independence 13

Chapter 4 Survey Responses: Blue-Collar Workers 16

Chapter 5 Survey Responses: White-Collar Professionals......... 46

Chapter 6 Survey Responses: Management Professionals........ 104

Chapter 7 Survey Responses: White-Collar Executives 127

Chapter 8 Emotional Intelligence 157

Chapter 9 Definitions 171

Chapter 10 Let's Reimagine.. 177

References.. 181

DEFINITIONS

Successful: Ramsey (2021) indicated that different people can define success very differently. Success is defined as one pursuing one's life purpose and passion. Success is a personal choice.

Introvert: Jung (1921) indicated that introverts are drawn to the inner world of thought and feeling. Cain (2012) noted that introverts work slowly and deliberately. Cain (2012) posited that introverts and extroverts differ in their level of outside stimulation.

DEDICATIONS AND THANKS

This book is dedicated to the many individuals who are struggling to be their authentic selves. If you are an introverted or extroverted person, please *be true to yourself.* This book is dedicated to my family and friends, who continue to push and inspire me to be my authentic self. From the bottom of my heart, I would like to take this time to publicly say thank you for believing in me.

To my wife, Lora Ramsey, thank you for being my rock and solid foundation. You have been there with me from the beginning of this book to its completion. Thank you for your encouragement and insight. Thank you for being a great lady, wife, and mother. Thank you for being authentic and real. I love you deeply.

To my parents, Florence and Minor C. Ramsey, Jr., thank you for your excellent examples of hard work and sacrifice. You instilled in me a great thirst for learning and growing. Thank you from the bottom of my heart.

To my daughters, Bri, Loren, and Taylor. I love each of you. I am very proud of you. Each of you is very smart, beautiful, caring, and wise. I pray that you will read this book and grow to your fullest potential.

To my granddaughter, Azaria La'Nay Ramsey; you are my gift. I pray that you will read this book and grow into the beautiful, smart, intelligent, and wise young lady God has ordained you to become. Always remember that your Paw Paw Len loves you.

To my sisters, Renee and Regina, you are my source of truth. You keep me grounded and centered. You allow me to text and talk with you daily. Thank you for your love, support, and encouragement. I love you.

To my past teachers (both good and not so good), thank you for your gift of teaching. Thank you for inspiring me to learn, grow, and expand my territories. I respect the work each of you do daily. Keep inspiring the next generation as you did with me.

INTERESTING QUOTES

Elizabeth Gilbert noted, "Embrace the glorious mess that you are."

Pastor Kenneth Duke said, "God gives strength to weak people."

Thomas Paine noted, "That which we obtain too easily, we esteem too lightly. It is dearness only which gives everything its value. Heaven knows how to put a proper price on its goods."

Stephen R. Covey posited that "self-growth is tender; it's holy ground. There's no greater investment."

T. S. Eliot indicated, "We must not cease from exploration and the end of all our exploring will be to arrive where we began and to know the place for the first time."

Aristotle said, "We are what we repeatedly do. Excellence, then, is not an act, but a habit."

A popular maxim says, "Sow a thought, reap an action; sow an action, reap a habit; sow a habit, reap a character; sow a character, reap a destiny."

CHAPTER 1

INTRODUCTION

When I first started this book, I was focused on how being an introvert can hurt one's chances of success in life and the global workplace. However, after several interviews with many successful introverts, this myopic way of thinking was gradually replaced with the thinking that being a successful introverted person was highly probable. However, the aspects of introverted individuals needed to be defined more precisely.

I started to reflect on my childhood and younger years of life. I realized I was an introvert as well. Over my life, I've worked very hard to push myself to be an extroverted individual and provide for my family. However, my primary moods are introversion and accommodation. These qualities can be both good and bad. From a positive standpoint, they enable me to get to know others at a deeper level. I'm able to form bonds quickly and deeply. On many occasions, complete strangers have shared their inner fears, dislikes, and loves with me. When this first started happening to me, I was somewhat taken aback. However, after it kept happening, I realized I had to use this "superpower" to be of service to others. I realized that many people are very introverted and unable to truly express themselves verbally. As such, we need individuals who are willing to be the "world interpreters" for this group of extremely introverted people.

In this book, I will explore the connections between success and introversion. In addition, I will show the correlations between emotional intelligence and success. Also, I will discuss how success can be achieved with the proper steps and emotional support from mentors, coaches, and so forth. However, the success journey is very different for each of us. It doesn't matter whether we are introverted or extroverted. We all must work at becoming our better selves in a daily and intentional way. Let's get to it.

Laney (2002) posited that introversion is "at its root a type of temperament. It is not the same as shyness or having a withdrawn personality." Laney (2002) asserted that "introversion is not pathological. It is also not something you can change. But you can learn to work with it, not against it."

Miyazaki noted that modern scientists tend to associate introverted people with people who desire time for themselves, are drained by social interactions, are introspective, favor writing over speaking, and tend to need only a small group of friends (Miyazaki 2021).

Swiss psychiatrist Carl Jung observed that introversion is "a mode of psychological orientation where the movement of energy is toward the inner world," while extroversion is the opposite (Buelow 2015). Extroverted people seek intensive contact with the outer world, engaging socially with others, and introverts are often directed inward, to the inner world, to the inner thoughts and feelings. A lot of research has shown that introverted people are usually seen as comforters and analytical types who prefer to work alone rather than in groups, who recharge energy from ideas in their inner world or by spending time being alone; they often get exhausted by social situations (Buelow 2015).

In early 1960, the German psychologist Han Eysenck added to Jung's theories through biological research the definitions of *introversion* and *extroversion*. His research has shown that the personality traits of introverts and extroverts are determined not only psychologically but also biologically. Eysenck noted that introverts have "naturally high cortical arousal, which means they reached their stimulation saturation point much more quickly than did extroverts." Kent (2006) noted, "Cortical arousal increases wakefulness, vigilance, muscle tone, heart rate, and minute ventilation," so if an introverted person exceeds the amount of external input coming his or her way, then it will push him or her into the realm of anxiety and overstimulation. This answers the question of why introverted people easily get exhausted by social situations. Kent (2006) explained that extroverted people tend to seek stimulation from social activities to raise their naturally low levels of cortical arousal, while introverts tend to avoid social situations to reduce their high levels of cortical arousal. Modern science has also found that introverted people often take in more information than extroverted people do. Magnetic resonance imaging has shown that introverted people carry blood flow to the forebrain faster than extroverted people do. This part of the brain is involved in thinking and problem-solving. That is why introverted people are so easily overwhelmed—all the information that suddenly floods in makes them feel overstimulated (Kent 2006).

Jung classifies the two groups of introversion and extroversion based on how they recharge their energies. Introverts prefer environments with little or even minimal stimulation, he says, and they need time alone to recharge. To replenish their energy, introverted people need to limit the number of social influences from the external world and draw energy from their internal ideas, thoughts, and emotions. So it's very important for introverted people to balance their lives and spend time alone and outside equally.

Kendra (2020) posited that some people feel introversion and shyness in the same way, but that is completely wrong. Introversion is a personality—patterns of thoughts, feelings, and behaviors—that make a person unique (Kendra 2020). Shyness is an emotion generated from outside influences. An introverted person may appear to be withdrawn and shy; however, this may not always be the case (Carrigan 1960). Shy people usually feel uncomfortable when they are in social situations, especially when they are surrounded by a lot of people. They often feel anxious and lack confidence. Their hearts may beat quicker, and they may get a stomachache. They may tend to ignore social events because they don't like the negative feelings that take over their thoughts and body when they participate in outdoor activities around many people (Rachel 2020).

Introverted people also prefer to skip social events, but this is because they feel more energized or comfortable doing things on their own or with one or two other people. Introverts are easily drained just by having endless talk or even by being in a large group of people. Introverts don't choose to avoid social events because they have strong negative reactions to larger gatherings the way shy people do; they just prefer being alone or in very small groups to control the amount of stimulation they might receive (Rachel 2020).

Carl Jung noted that no one is completely introverted or extroverted, but he hypothesized that people are born with a tendency to move constantly between being very introverted and being extroverted. Jung believed that each person carries traits of the two personalities. He described this by saying that "introversion and extroversion [are] personality extremes at the two ends of a continuum." The fact is that if a person is able to change between two personalities, depending on the situation, then he or she can completely integrate into society in the best way.

However, Jung also realized that the human mind doesn't usually work that way. Most people's minds tend to lean to either one side or the other. Those people who can perfectly balance introversion and extroversion are called "ambiverts." Jung concluded that we all have a "natural niche," a place between two ends of the continuum where we function best; and except for either extreme, any place on the continuum is healthy (Marti 2002). We see this theory is used in a lot of research in psychology and is also the basis for showing the differences between introversion and extroversion.

One of the main differences between introverted and extroverted people is how they recharge their energy. Two other differences particularly affect their lives and work. Laney (2002) indicated that those are the way they react to external stimulation and how they approach and process knowledge and experiences. It is the response and tolerance to external stimulation—toward other people or in a certain situation—and the ability to analyze, learn, and process information. Introverts are often directed to their inner thoughts and feelings; therefore, what introverted people find interesting might be boring to extroverted people. Introverted people enjoy learning and react to things in a profound way, making conclusions intentional rather than spontaneous.

Extroverted people, however, like to experience a lot of things but don't necessarily feel that they need to dig too deep into those things. From an experience of external stimulation, introverted people tend to dig deep. If they can focus on one or two things, like reading a book or doing a project, they can do very well. But if four or five more things are going on, they will get overwhelmed. Introverted people are often quite sensitive to social situations, and exposure to new things from the outside can make them easily overstimulated. Laney (2002) stated that introverted people often subconsciously try to control their experiences of overstimulation by limiting the amount of information they take in as much as possible.

Extroverted people like to experience a lot of activities. Opposite to introverts, extroverts are overwhelmed by inner activities, like reading a book in the library, and they like to recharge by enjoying a lively environment where the action is. By recharging, extroverted people can increase their energy, while those introverted decrease their external stimulation. By processing new knowledge, as the author mentioned, introverted people can do very well if they focus on only one or two things at a time and tend to learn thoroughly with new knowledge; they observe external experiences and then reflect and expand that information. That is also one of the main reasons they just need to have a group of close friends, because they feel comfortable being with people they know. They place a high value on "quality" over "quantity." Laney (2002) states that when introverted people focus on something, it's hard to pull them out of their thought. Often introverted people achieve the best results when they work in an undisturbed and quiet setting; they disappear into a state of deep focus or flow and feel very uncomfortable when being interrupted. She also said that concentration requires a lot of energy, and that explains the reason why they can focus on only one or two things at a time. Extroverted people like to experience a lot, knowing a little bit about everything; but because they are often overwhelmed by inner activities, they skip to expand deeply with the new experience and continue to the next one.

People often assume that introverts don't like being leaders because of their quiet personalities, and their silence is often seen as a weakness in today's society, where the loudest voice often decides success. The fact is that introverted people can be great leaders; they just "do not get the chance to do so." Having a quiet working style, tending to be very careful, and being less likely to take great risks are some examples of the strengths of introverted leaders. They can do well in many areas if they learn how to use their skills properly. Kahnweiler (2009) mentions in her book that introverted leaders in businesses often approach their introversion as a business problem and learn what behaviors are good and which aren't. Then they develop a strategy and execute it, finding their own ways to adapt. "Many introverted traits that are generally looked down upon in the world of business can prove to be beneficial," so instead of trying to eliminate or hide the abilities they have, the introverted should tap into them (Kahnweilter 2009).

Kahnweilter (2009) notes that introverts don't have "people skills." In businesses, leaders often choose people with charisma and confidence; "people skills" are considered necessary for effective leadership. People are often chosen for leadership roles due to the characteristics introverts often have difficulty showing regularly. Much research proves that though highly charismatic people are often nominated for leadership roles, having high charisma doesn't mean having a high success rate at work. Research also shows that introverted leaders outperformed leaders hired solely because of their charming personalities. Indeed, introverted people don't possess as much charisma as extroverted people, but this has absolutely no effect on their leadership ability. Kahnweiler (2013) posits that introverts are bad communicators. However, one of the strengths introverted people have is their listening skills. This helps them to "understand what's going on around them: what people are thinking and feeling, threads of themes, and even what key pieces of the puzzle might be missing" (Kahnweiler 2013). Introverted people often take a while to analyze and process the information they have just received before giving an answer. Introverted people tend to like to think carefully.

Kahnweiler (2013) indicates that introverts tend to consider different situations and simulate the possibilities in their heads before coming to a decision. This way of thinking makes their decisions more certain, often leading to a misunderstanding that they aren't interested in the situation. However, as a leader, this allows introverted people to "present their ideas in a more concrete, well-thought-out, and lucid manner." Kahnweiler (2013) notes that introverts don't like collaborating. As the author has mentioned, introverted people tend to be overstimulated when engaging in social situations for a long period, and they often work quite effectively when alone because of their high concentration at work. However, that doesn't mean they are ineffective when in a group. In fact, their ability to think and analyze the situation carefully before concluding is a plus and can absolutely bring great help in case the whole group is in a crisis. Caring about employees and customers or understanding the dark side of problems is an essential trait of a leader. Introverted leaders are great observers and listeners because they pay attention to every little detail. They listen to what people have to say and make a point only when it is worth it. In addition, they aren't interested in being the center of attention, always put the spotlight on others, and appreciate ideas and suggestions from people around them (Martinuzzi 2013). Dubrin (2002) noted that introverted leaders have the ability to "inspire confidence and support among the people who are needed to achieve organizational goal."

The definition of *leadership* has changed a lot over time. Originally, a leader meant someone who encouraged his or her team members to work together toward a common goal. Now *leader* is the word that describes a charismatic, daring person who can rule the whole team (Daron 2020). The second definition of *leadership* has some traits that are quite familiar to those who carry extroversion traits. There have been large amounts of research over the centuries about what traits make an effective leader; however, so far the answer to that question still isn't final. Leaders in every business have their own way of managing, and it's nearly impossible to understand the common characteristics all leaders have. In addition, the success of a business not only comes from the leader alone but also depends on many different factors.

Dubrin (2002) posited that the effectiveness of a leader is based on three factors:

- The leader's characteristics, behavior, and style
- Group members' characteristics and behavior
- The internal and external environment

The leader's characteristics and behavior refer to values from within, such as dynamism, confidence, and problem-solving, all of which make him or her a leader. Leadership style refers to how he or she approaches work and employees. For example, approach work with caution and always be strict with employees. Group member characteristics and behavior refer to the attributes of team members that can affect the effectiveness of leadership efforts. For example, a leader will have a high probability of success if he or she has talented and dedicated subordinates.

Dinh (2022) indicated that introverted people can be not only leaders but also even excellent leaders in an organization. The problem lies in how people envision a successful leader. More than the average success, introverted leaders who know how to optimize their weaknesses are great leaders. Collins (2001) posited that after studying and documenting the activities of thousands of businesses, it has been concluded that successful companies often have exceptionally successful leaders. Collins called it by the title of "Level 5 Leadership." Some of the characteristics of "Level 5 Leadership" include humility, patience, and modesty, which are dominant traits of introverts. In addition, Goleman (2006) indicated that a good leader has traits that are consistent or similar to the personality of an introverted individual.

CHAPTER 2

LEADER TRAITS

Today, as I write this book, my dear auntie Alice Tillis passed away only a few hours ago. She passed on March 19, 2021. Her family and friends will greatly miss her. Auntie Alice made everyone feel very special and welcome. She did so in a nonthreatening and personable manner. She knew how to listen and effectively respond. She may have learned these leadership traits and attributes from her mother and father. Moreover, my auntie Alice was a great leader to me and many others. She knew how to influence and get the best out of others. To me, this trait is a mark of a great leader. As such, for this book I will explore and research the traits and attributes of a great leader through the lens of introversion and extroversion tendencies with correlations to emotional intelligence. This book may be used to study and understand what it takes to be a successful and effective global leader if you are an introverted or extroverted individual.

In addition, I believed my auntie possessed a high degree of emotional intelligence. This book will delve into the topic of emotional intelligence as well.

What made these leaders so great? What did they possess that made them such great leaders? Were they born as leaders? Were they taught to be leaders? Which attributes made them better leaders than others? Let's consider the leadership approach of the following great leaders:

1. Dr. Martin Luther King Jr. (global leader)
2. Abraham Lincoln (American president and global leader)
3. Mahatma Gandhi (civil rights and global leader)
4. Nelson Mandela (civil rights and global leader)
5. Margaret Thatcher (prime minister)
6. Madam C. J. Walker (entrepreneur and leader)
7. Fannie Lou Hamer (civil rights leader)

Great leaders inspire and motivate others with their words and actions. Let us explore leaders like Dr. King, Abraham Lincoln, Mahatma Gandhi, King David, King Solomon, and other great leaders through the annals of history. Each of these leaders was able to inspire and motivate others with his or her words and actions. Each of their actions may have been different; however, each of them possessed the traits and attributes of a great leader. Each of them was either introverted or extroverted. However, they overcame their fears and became great leaders. How were they able to overcome their fears and phobias? What motivated them to want to change and leave a great mark on our global world? Which characteristics or attributes helped or assisted them in their journey to be great? Whom did they surround themselves with to push them to be greater? The author posits that they kept the company of others who pushed them. They held themselves to a higher standard. They wouldn't accept failure as an option. The goal was a success.

The introverted individual can be highly functional and effective in a global work environment. Therefore, it's imperative that global organizations create space and accommodate those individuals who are bent toward introversion tendencies. The author noted that one's introversion may hinder or hurt one in the global marketplace. Fortunately, based on empirical and literature evidence, the author's hypothesis has been proved false and null. The introverted individual can thrive very well in the global marketplace of ideas.

Popoola and Karadas (2022) noted that employees who want to successfully achieve their goals must possess a characteristic called "grit" (Duckworth et al. 2007). Popoola and Karadas (2022) posited that one's passion, objective, and ability to self-regulate a wide array of abstract goals far into the future remain that critical ingredient with grit. Duckworth et al. (2007) indicated that employees with a higher level of grit tend to be more focused for a longer period on activities, even when they are presented with tests, hindrances, and harsh conditions (Popoola and Karadas 2022).

Chamorro-Premuzic (2019) indicated that people tend to equate leadership with the bad behavior of "overconfidence." Unfortunately, this quality is a bad signal for bad or poor leadership. In addition, this quality is more common with average men than with average women. This results in a pathological system that rewards the incompetence of men and punishes women for their competence. This entire leader-evaluation criteria process needs to be reexamined and replaced with a more relevant and effective process (Chamorro-Premuzic 2019). Once this system is replaced, it will help not only women but also everyone else. It will allow better leaders to be picked (Chamorro-Premuzic 2019).

Akhtar et al. (2015) posited that work engagement appears to be a critical antecedent or predictor of organizational outcomes such as citizenship behavior and employee productivity. To understand the correlation between the antecedents of work engagement, Petrides and Furnham (2003) examined the differences in personality traits possessed by more- or less-engaged employees. A comprehensive and exhausting understanding of a wide range of traits appears to be lacking. Some of these lacking traits are the role of emotional intelligence (EI) and contextualized measures of personality. The definition of work engagement consists of activation and energy (Xanthopoulou et al. 2009).

Akhtar et al. (2015) indicated that when looking at various predictors alone, trait EI predicted engagement even after controlling the variance of personality factors and age. Trait EI's unique contribution in predicting work engagement beyond demographics and personality. This important finding suggests that emotionally intelligent employees are more likely to be engaged at work regardless of age or gender. Akhtar et al. (2015) posited that by understanding predictors of engagement, an organization can select employees that are high on personality traits such as EI, openness, extraversion, conscientiousness, adjustment, ambition, and interpersonal sensitivity. An organization should include these characteristics in its selection criteria and process. These characteristics may improve the likelihood of high-performing job candidates. In addition, Akhtar et al. (2015) noted that most organizations are increasing engagement efforts by focusing on changes related to the demands of the job and the limited resources. Organizations can maximize their resources by being able to better predict employees' engagement earlier in the selection process.

CHAPTER 3

HYPER INDEPENDENCE

Oelwang (2022) noted that we are programmed to prioritize individual accomplishment over deep connections and partnerships with others. The glorification of hyperindividualism has unfortunate consequences of a crisis of loneliness. In addition, we fear the difference of others instead of celebrating these differences. Too many people have forgotten basic civility and kindness. When we prioritize individualism, there is ever-present racism, climate change, and inequality. Society misses out on opportunities to achieve greater collective good. Oelwang (2022) posited that a 2020 study from the Pew Research Center revealed that 57 percent of Americans think most people only look out for themselves and don't help others.

Blevin, Stackhouse, and Dionne (2022) indicated that extroversion is a personality trait characterized by assertion, dominance, social prowess, and outgoingness; and being the focal point of attention (Ashton and Lee 2009; Lee and Ashton 2004) is one of the most studied personality traits used to understand workplace outcomes. Bono and Judge (2004) posited that the literature studying personality has focused mainly on the benefits of extroversion at multiple levels of analysis with findings supporting the important role of extroversion in organizations at the individual leadership and team levels that is Barrick and Mount (1991); however, extroverted individuals represent only a subset of the population, according to Grant (2013). Some studies suggest that more than half the population may be viewed as having a personality that wouldn't be considered extroverted.

Cain (2012) noted there may be potential benefits associated with extraversion and introversion alike, but the literature appears to largely support the benefits associated with extroverts, showing only a little attention devoted to understanding how introverts may positively shape workplace outcomes.

Blevin, Stackhouse, and Dionne (2022) noted that extroversion has benefited from substantial interest by organizational scholars; it's been highlighted how introversion benefits are largely neglected as a topic of study in the workplace, with estimates showing introverts may represent as many as two-thirds of the workplace in some countries. Cain (2012) posited that it's time to start understanding both when and how introverts can continue to add value within their workplaces. However, this step forward requires the more direct acknowledgment of the many unseen and unheard contributions owned to introverted individuals; what should be studied in future research are the potential advantages of introverts at multiple levels within organizations individual and team environments and beyond while also informing any interested organization leaders' teens or individuals of the power of both extroverted and introverted individuals (Blevin, Stackhouse, and Dionne 2022).

Bhati (2022) posited that hyper-independent people tend to want to do everything without the help of anyone. They aren't willing to ask for help because they feel no one can do things at their level. Therefore, hyper-independent persons do everything by and for themselves. When one does everything alone, this can be very exhausting. "Anything in excess is bad, even being too independent can harm you" (Bhati 2022).

Bhati (2022) noted that hyper-independent people make their decisions based on their past experiences. Hyper-independent people may have been traumatized by a past experience. Based on this experience, the hyper-independent person tends to look inward. Bhati (2022) indicated that when one experiences emotional or physical trauma, he or she resorts to hyper-independence. The hyper-independent person isn't willing to take any chances or risks with others. He or she has trust issues. This is problematic in relationships both at work and personally. "Hyper independence and relationships do not go well together. All kinds of relationships suffer if one of them is a hyper independent person" (Bhati 2022).

Bhati (2022) posited that one can overcome hyper independence in two ways. They are the task-trust-ask method and the check-your-ego approach. With the task-trust-ask method, the hyper-independent person must do three things:

1. Assign tasks to someone else, even those the person can do himself or herself.
2. After the task is assigned and completed, the hyper-independent person will start to build trust.
3. Once the trust is built, it becomes easier for the hyper-independent person to ask for help.

Bhati (2022) noted that with the check-your-ego approach, the hyper-independent person must be able to evaluate and regulate his or her ego. The hyper-independent person must be able questions his or her thoughts.

Collins (2001) noted that level 5 leaders possess two qualities: humility and will. Level 5 leaders are willing to check their egos and work toward the greater good of the organization or company. Level 5 leaders are ambitious. However, they put the interests of the organization above their selfish motives. Collins (2001) posited that embodies all five layers of the leadership pyramid. They are able to make productive contributions with talent, knowledge, skills, and good work habits. In addition, the level 5 leader is able to build enduring greatness through a blend of both personal humility and professional will.

CHAPTER 4

SURVEY RESPONSES: BLUE-COLLAR WORKERS

Survey Responses: Blue-Collar Workers

Emotional Intelligence and Introversion/Extroversion Tendency Interview (40 Questions)

Send to Dr. Reginald Ramsey, PhD, MBA, CISA, @ <u>HRTC1906@ gmail.com</u>

Name:_____Black/Female/Professional_____

Response Date: ___5/25/2022_____

1. What is your official job title? Waitress/cleaner

2. How long have you been in your current role? Three years

3. What attributes or skills helped you to reach your current career level? Customer service skills

4. What does your typical day entail? Please elaborate as much as possible. Lots of people, cleaning, music, and socializing

5. How many hours do you work per week? Twenty-five to thirty-three

6. What advice would you give to someone who wants to be in your position someday? Don't give up; keep focused. You have to get the job done.

7. What has been the role of mentors or coaches in your career advancement? They help to motivate; they help me to deal with people. They are active listeners.

8. How many mentors do you have or have had over your career? Six

9. How often do you speak or communicate with your mentor or mentors? Daily for five years straight, twice per year

10. How do you balance your work with your private life? Do what needs to be done ... Do what needs to be done.

11. How often do you set goals? Twice per month

12. What type of goals do you set (yearly, monthly, and so forth)? Yearly, monthly for my kids

13. How long have you been working in the market space? Since 2011

14. What was your first job? Firehouse Subs

15. What valuable lessons have you learned over your career? Don't trust everybody. Stay focused. Show you're friendly. Don't be gullible.

16. What type of spiritual life do you have? I grew up in a spiritual home. I believe in a God.

17. Do you attend or engage in any religious activities? Yes

18. What role has emotional intelligence played in your career progression? I get vibes off the other person's vibes … His or her face tells it all …

19. What are some unwritten rules or norms you learned from being in a white-collar environment? Showing identity because of skin color

20. Did your parents or grandparents work in a white-collar setting? Yes or no? Yes

21. Did your parents or grandparents teach you how to navigate a white-collar working environment? Yes

22. What did your parents or grandparents teach you about working in a white-collar environment? Make people accept you as you are.

23. How did you learn about these unwritten rules or norms (observation, mentors, mistakes)? All of the above

24. Currently, how many individuals do you mentor? Three

25. How often do you listen to or read about successful individuals? All the time; I observe my family members.

26. What role has self-talk played in your career success? It has done a lot for me. I tell myself that I'm beautiful. There is nothing—nobody can make or break you.

27. How do you motivate yourself each day? I get up and do this. I focus on my kids.

28. What are some of your hobbies? Singing, dancing, designing

29. Do you believe in the PIE model for career success? Yes

30. How often do you exercise? Three times per week

31. How much time do you take off each year to recharge your batteries? Four days per year

32. May I use your name in the book? Keep confidential.

33. Whom would you recommend I interview for this book? NA

34. How would you characterize yourself (either introverted or extroverted)? Introverted

35. What introverted or extroverted qualities do you daily display to the general public?

    Introverted—I like being alone. I love reading, studying, writing music, and thinking. I get more done.

36. On a scale of one to ten, with ten being the easiest, how easy is it for you to start a conversation with a stranger? Six or seven

37. On a scale of one to ten, with ten being the easiest, how easy is it for you to network with others in the workplace? In the middle: six

38. What are some tools you use to maintain relationships with others? Being honest, always being honest with others

39. What is your preferred method of communication (email, in person, phone, and so forth)? Texting or email

40. How much energy does it take for you to navigate the corporate or white-collar working environment? It takes a lot at the beginning.

Emotional Intelligence and Introversion/Extroversion Tendency Interview (40 Questions)

Send to Dr. Reginald Ramsey, PhD, MBA, CISA, @ <u>HRTC1906@ gmail.com</u>

Name: <u>Black/Female/Professional</u>

Response Date: Friday, July 22, 2022

1. What is your official job title? Academic tutor (since retirement)

2. How long have you been in your current role? 1.5 years

3. What attributes or skills helped you to reach your current career level? Technology. I was able to use the left and right brain. I do web design.

4. What does your typical day entail? Please elaborate as much as possible. I assist the teachers and students at a middle school.

5. How many hours do you work per week? Thirty-four to thirty-six

6. What advice would you give to someone who wants to be in your position someday? Be willing to give back to the community. Develop a love for math.

7. What has been the role of mentors or coaches in your career advancement? I never had any official mentors or coaches.

8. How many mentors do you have or have had over your career? None

9. How often do you speak or communicate with your mentor or mentors? NA

10. How do you balance your work with your private life? As a single woman in the corporate world, I would stay until 6 p.m. I had no family or responsibilities. After my child was born, I had to pick up my son from day care. My supervisors allowed me the space to get my son.

11. How often do you set goals? I don't set goals; I just go with the flow.

12. What type of goals do you set (yearly, monthly, and so forth)?

    I really haven't been a goal setter since leaving my job with IBM in 1974. I wasn't planning to leave IBM, but a friend convinced me to take an interview just to see what was out there. I did, and I was hired. I left IBM, making 25 percent more that before the interview. So my mindset was to go with the flow. New opportunities would show up. Only once was I disappointed. But just recently I did set goals for products to be sold on my Etsy shop later this year; it's nothing formal, just a plan with a couple of dates in mind.

13. How long have you been working in the market space?

    I've been a paper crafter since 2014, and I've had the Etsy shop since 2015. I created it just to see what would happen with little effort.

14. What was your first job?

    For my first job out of school, IBM hired me as a software engineer in 1972. But in high school, my very first job was as a cashier in a supermarket in the Black community. Wow! I think my lessons in people skills and people management started then.

15. What valuable lessons have you learned over your career?

    I am the one responsible for me and my career. I am the one who makes the choices of who I want to be and what I want to be doing with integrity. I've had too many managers who were without integrity. I also learned how threatened white male coworkers are of an educated Black woman. Fortunately, those attitudes didn't dominate my career.

16. What type of spiritual life do you have?

I have a very active spiritual life. I'm not as involved with my Unity church as I was before the pandemic, where I managed their online streaming of services twice a month. Now I'm involved in a group that practices an ancient Hawaiian forgiveness practice. I love attending art workshops that are spiritually inspired. I've been going to them sporadically for about ten years.

17. Do you attend or engage in any religious activities?

I attend church online most Sundays now. I'm happy avoiding traffic and dealing with parking issues. I was active with a very loving spiritual group. But when COVID happened, a QAnon person took it over, and I no longer found it inspirational.

18. What role has emotional intelligence played in your career progression?

I learned a lot about managing political and backstabbing situations. I learned early on to document. I've never been one to keep silent when there is wrongdoing. I have had managers who supported me, which was helpful.

19. What are some unwritten rules or norms you learned from being in a white-collar environment?

Document everything, listen carefully, watch body language, and observe the people in the room, not just the person speaking. Their facial expressions and body language tell a lot. I also learned to let management know when things were not going well as soon as I discovered a problem. I had managers who hid problems from management.

20. Did your parents or grandparents work in a white-collar setting? Yes or no? My dad did.

21. Did your parents or grandparents teach you how to navigate a white-collar working environment?

No. My dad didn't talk about his challenges as the only Black civil engineer or even when he became a lawyer. I do know that the company where he worked for thirteen years refused to hire him into their law department when he passed the bar, so he was forced to work elsewhere. He worked for only three companies in his entire career.

22. What did your parents or grandparents teach you about working in a white-collar environment?

Nothing at all. I think my dad didn't feel my job was similar enough to his to realize I may have experienced some of the same issues. But I feel deeply that he just never wanted to talk about them.

23. How did you learn about these unwritten rules or norms (observation, mentors, mistakes)? Observation, experience, making mistakes

24. Currently, how many individuals do you mentor?

I don't consider myself a real mentor to some of my students I've tried to mentor. There seems to be a lot of resistance to doing what is a challenge with so many of their peers around them, who aren't motivated either. I tutor, but I see teachers who've been teaching for twenty-five and thirty years basically give up on some students. They say the atmosphere is the worst they've ever seen. But I think no one knows how to reach these kids, most of whom were isolated by the pandemic. When they returned to school last year, they really didn't seem to care. Maybe some of it is because none of them failed because of the change to virtual learning. I think this may have given them a false sense of security. But I still try because none of us really knows what's going on in their home life.

25. How often do you listen to or read about successful individuals?

I mostly watch interviews on news, podcasts, and talk shows. I find myself not reading so much anymore just to read. I now read how-to info. I listen to audiobooks in the car instead of reading. I love hearing about the experiences of others.

26. What role has self-talk played in your career success?

I never had the problem of negative self-talk. I do very deep thinking and analyzing when I want to accomplish something. Since I've never had a mentor, I just do a lot of observing and research as necessary. I have found that educating myself is my best motivation to become the best and put what I've learned in action at my work.

27. How do you motivate yourself each day?

I have my own projects that motivate me and inspire me to learn more and then figure out how I will use what I know. Working on achieving the Apple Teacher Certification is key because I've already been a successful Apple Mac teacher for adults. I know something will show up that will allow me to use it.

28. What are some of your hobbies?

I make handmade greeting cards and taught classes for a few years until the shutdown. It's so relaxing, and I believe it helps me remain cancer free from stress.

29. Do you believe in the PIE model for career success?

Well, after doing a Google search to see what it is, I think it's a great concept. But I feel it requires more integrity than many in business have, require, or use.

30. How often do you exercise?

I have a dog, so I do one long walk and about half of that as a second walk most days when the heat and humidity aren't so bad for him. I'm thinking of doing what other dog owners do: take a longer walk alone and leave the dog at home. Without the sniff factor, I can go a lot farther and faster. Just recently I became interested in maybe getting a fitness coach.

31. How much time do you take off each year to recharge your batteries?

Once or twice a year, I travel, which is a way to recharge. Each trip has had a purpose of either reconnecting with sister friends or traveling with family. Both were very enjoyable.

32. May I use your name in the book?

Sure!

33. Whom would you recommend I interview for this book?

I have two Black women in mind. I can reach out to them to see if they are open to it.

34. How would you characterize yourself (either introverted or extroverted)?

Definitely extroverted

35. What introverted or extroverted qualities do you daily display to the general public?

When I travel alone, I don't want to talk to anyone. Otherwise, I'm open to interesting conversations. But I prefer starting with fairly neutral topics.

36. On a scale of one to ten, with ten being easiest, how easy is it for you to start a conversation with a stranger?

Five: I need to know we have something in common first. Some topics aren't great topics to initiate with strangers, like religion and politics.

37. On a scale of one to ten, with ten being easiest, how easy is it for you to network with others in the workplace?

Five: Although I like the people I work with now, at the school I don't see us having common interests. Being in the school environment is different from the white-collar experiences I've had. But they have their politics too.

Ten: When I was in corporate, I mostly networked through the Society of Women Engineers. We had common issues and interests. But even they didn't address racial issues on a large scale. I connected with other Black women engineers in the organization, but we never addressed workplace issues … That's interesting now that I think of it.

38. What are some tools you use to maintain relationships with others?

I text and email, and I occasionally call. I'm finding that restarting since we were all isolated is almost a new art form.

39. What is your preferred method of communication (email, in person, phone, and so forth)?

    It depends on who it is. There are two women I have no career or social history in common with, but we try to meet for lunch once a month. We have pleasant conversations and are somewhat like minded about politics and others we know socially, but I have no spiritual connection with them. Those I do have a spiritual connection with—we don't socialize outside of artistic workshops. Hmmm ...

40. How much energy does it take for you to navigate the corporate or white-collar working environment?

    Now, not anymore. As I mentioned, working at the school is the first job I've had in fifty years where my gender or race isn't an issue. But the educational environment from where I sit isn't as political or stressful as it is for the teachers and other staff.

    When I was healing from stage 4 cancer, which had metastasized, and my doctor put me on disability (which led to my retirement), that was the best thing that happened to me.

    I spoke to my holistic doctor and asked her how I had ended up with breast cancer, which wasn't on either side of my family. She said it was from stress and that many more women without a family history are now being diagnosed. Once I navigated the disability process, I felt freer to do what made me happy and do what I wanted.

    I don't miss corporate *at all*!

Emotional Intelligence and Introversion/Extroversion Tendency Interview (40 Questions)

Send to Dr. Reginald Ramsey, PhD, MBA, CISA, @ HRTC1906@ gmail.com

Name:__Black/Male/Professional_____

Response Date: ____July 7, 2022_____

1. What is your official job title? I'm looking for a job; I just graduated from a community college. I start my bachelor's degree in the fall of 2022.

2. How long have you been in your current role? Three years

3. What attributes or skills helped you to reach your current career level? Persistence and getting it done; I focused on getting the job done.

4. What does your typical day entail? Please elaborate as much as possible. Physical classes, class to class, and courses online. I had to stay on it. I wrote papers. I learned not to procrastinate.

5. How many hours do you work per week? Approximately two to three hours per day

6. What advice would you give to someone who wants to be in your position someday? Go to a community college; it is less expensive and will keep the debt low.

7. What has been the role of mentors or coaches in your career advancement? Mentors have helped me a lot; I learned about how money works. That is useful information. I also learned leadership skills, presentation skills, and how to shop for clothes.

8. How many mentors do you have or have had over your career? Five

9. How often do you speak or communicate with your mentor or mentors? Often

10. How do you balance your work with your private life? I was working at Walmart and my own business. I had to get it done. I learned time management.

11. How often do you set goals? Monthly

12. What type of goals do you set (yearly, monthly, and so forth)? I have monthly personal goals for acoustic guitar and piano. I play each day, practice, and read notes.

13. How long have you been working in the market space? Five years

14. What was your first job? Summer camp counselor

15. What valuable lessons have you learned over your career? "Don't compare yourself to someone who is great; compare yourself to your yesterday" (Jim Rohm).

16. What type of spiritual life do you have? I pray and meditate.

17. Do you attend or engage in any religious activities? Yes, church

18. What role has emotional intelligence played in your career progression? I have learned how to keep myself in check and when to take a minute to calm down.

19. What are some unwritten rules or norms you learned from being in a white-collar environment? No one will talk about the classes you took.

20. Did your parents or grandparents work in a white-collar setting? Yes or no? Yes

21. Did your parents or grandparents teach you how to navigate a white-collar working environment? Yes.

22. What did your parents or grandparents teach you about working in a white-collar environment? Stay professional all the time.

23. How did you learn about these unwritten rules or norms (observation, mentors, mistakes)? Parents and mentors

24. Currently, how many individuals do you mentor? None

25. How often do you listen to or read about successful individuals? I listen to Wayne Dyer and Jim Rohn.

26. What role has self-talk played in your career success? A big role. Words matter. It helps me with my confidence.

27. How do you motivate yourself each day? I think about the end results.

28. What are some of your hobbies? Reading, biking, making music (R&B)

29. Do you believe in the PIE model for career success? Yes

30. How often do you exercise? Three to four times per week

31. How much time do you take off each year to recharge your batteries? NA

32. May I use your name in the book? Keep confidential.

33. Whom would you recommend I interview for this book?

34. How would you characterize yourself (either introverted or extroverted)? Introverted

35. What introverted or extroverted qualities do you daily display to the general public?

    I'm introverted—thinking.

36. On a scale of one to ten, with ten being easiest, how easy is it for you to start a conversation with a stranger? Seven

37. On a scale of one to ten, with ten being easiest, how easy is it for you to network with others in the workplace? Seven

38. What are some tools you use to maintain relationships with others? Phone and email

39. What is your preferred method of communication (email, in person, phone, and so forth)? Phone for long talks

40. How much energy does it take for you to navigate the corporate or white-collar working environment? It's not too much a problem. It's important to stay respectful.

Emotional Intelligence and Introversion/Extroversion Tendency Interview (40 Questions)

Send to Dr. Reginald Ramsey, PhD, MBA, CISA, @ HRTC1906@ gmail.com

Name:____Female/Black/Profession_____

Response Date: ____5/18/2022_____

1. What is your official job title? Senior supervisor (call center)

2. How long have you been in your current role? Ten years

3. What attributes or skills helped you to reach your current career level? Customer service, problem-solving, staying to myself, staying in my own lane

4. What does your typical day entail? Please elaborate as much as possible. Problem-solving, taking complaints, listening

5. How many hours do you work per week? Twenty

6. What advice would you give to someone who wants to be in your position someday? Keep working hard, keep working on customer service skills, keep your numbers up, train others well.

7. What has been the role of mentors or coaches in your career advancement? Tell the good and bad; give constructive feedback.

8. How many mentors do you have or have had over your career? Three

9. How often do you speak or communicate with your mentor or mentors? Once per month

10. How do you balance your work with your private life? I keep them separate. I don't work at home; I don't mix the two.

11. How often do you set goals? I set work goals monthly, four goals per month.

12. What type of goals do you set (yearly, monthly, and so forth)? Monthly

13. How long have you been working in the market space? Since sixteen, about twenty-four years

14. What was your first job? Secretary

15. What valuable lessons have you learned over your career? I learned to listen completely, problem-solve, stick to the goal, and do your best.

16. What type of spiritual life do you have? Strong

17. Do you attend or engage in any religious activities? Yes

18. What role has emotional intelligence played in your career progression? A major role. I read people better. It helps to solve problems better.

19. What are some unwritten rules or norms you learned from being in a white-collar environment? Don't fraternize. Don't get into friendships. Don't drink.

20. Did your parents or grandparents work in a white-collar setting? Yes or no? Yes, my mom did.

21. Did your parents or grandparents teach you how to navigate a white-collar working environment? Yes

22. What did your parents or grandparents teach you about working in a white-collar environment? Go with the flow; learn the rules.

23. How did you learn about these unwritten rules or norms (observation, mentors, mistakes)? Mistakes and observations

24. Currently, how many individuals do you mentor? Five

25. How often do you listen to or read about successful individuals? All the time

26. What role has self-talk played in your career success? I treat people how I want to be treated.

27. How do you motivate yourself each day? Affirmations, prayer, God

28. What are some of your hobbies? Reading, writing, volunteering

29. Do you believe in the PIE model for career success? No. It is not written for people of color; it is written for different levels of employment.

30. How often do you exercise? Daily

31. How much time do you take off each year to recharge your batteries? I don't take time off.

32. May I use your name in the book? Keep confidential.

33. Whom would you recommend I interview for this book? NA

34. How would you characterize yourself (either introverted or extroverted)? Introverted

35. What introverted or extroverted qualities do you daily display to the general public?

    Introverted—I stay to myself. I stay at my desk.

36. On a scale of one to ten, with ten being easiest, how easy is it for you to start a conversation with a stranger? Ten

37. On a scale of one to ten, with ten being easiest, how easy is it for you to network with others in the workplace? Three

38. What are some tools you use to maintain relationships with others? Communications, text, email, motivational emails, encouragement

39. What is your preferred method of communication (email, in person, phone, and so forth)? Email, text, or phone

40. How much energy does it take for you to navigate the corporate or white-collar working environment? It is easy and not easy. It is hard for new people. It is easy for me.

Emotional Intelligence and Introversion/Extroversion Tendency Interview (40 Questions)

Send to Dr. Reginald Ramsey, PhD, MBA, CISA, @ HRTC1906@gmail.com

Name:___Black/Female/Professional _____

Response Date: ___July 5, 2022_____

1. What is your official job title? Interim program manager

2. How long have you been in your current role? Thirty days

3. What attributes or skills helped you to reach your current career level? Experience; education; the ability to adapt; understanding different mindsets; social, cultural, and emotional intelligence

4. What does your typical day entail? Please elaborate as much as possible. Attending meetings; reporting; collaborating; working with different leaders, staff, and team members; getting input from team members as appropriate

5. How many hours do you work per week? Forty

6. What advice would you give to someone who wants to be in your position someday? Be engaging. Show interests and genuine concern. Ask questions.

7. What has been the role of mentors or coaches in your career advancement? They give advice without being getting stabbed. They recommend how to implement projects.

8. How many mentors do you have or have had over your career? Four

9. How often do you speak or communicate with your mentor or mentors? Monthly. We discuss improvements and staffing. We have career-related discussions and talk about new opportunities.

10. How do you balance your work with your private life? I ensure that I get my to-do list done. I get it done before 5 p.m., two hours before leaving.

11. How often do you set goals? Not as often as I should; every six months there is a goal set (personal, work, or financial).

12. What type of goals do you set (yearly, monthly, and so forth)? Six-month goals

13. How long have you been working in the market space? Thirty-seven years

14. What was your first job? I worked at a fast-food establishment.

15. What valuable lessons have you learned over your career? I keep God first, family second. I always remember these two things when making major decisions.

16. What type of spiritual life do you have? I'm very spiritual; I have a relationship with God.

17. Do you attend or engage in any religious activities? Yes. I engage in church activities.

18. What role has emotional intelligence played in your career progression? It's a part of life. Don't let emotions control your responses; sixty high end.

19. What are some unwritten rules or norms you learned from being in a white-collar environment? Rules can change without notice. For example, in a meeting, someone made a statement about a rule. We changed this new rule. One has to adapt slowly. Pick your battles and choose wisely.

20. Did your parents or grandparents work in a white-collar setting? Yes or no? My mom worked at a restaurant; she was a cook.

21. Did your parents or grandparents teach you how to navigate a white-collar working environment? Watching her helped me to understand the value of work.

22. What did your parents or grandparents teach you about working in a white-collar environment? See above.

23. How did you learn about these unwritten rules or norms (observation, mentors, mistakes)? Mistakes, mentors

24. Currently, how many individuals do you mentor? None

25. How often do you listen to or read about successful individuals? Three times per week. I also do a Bible study.

26. What role has self-talk played in your career success? It has been a game changer; I encourage myself.

27. How do you motivate yourself each day? Self-talk and prayer

28. What are some of your hobbies? Riding motorcycles, sewing, writing

29. Do you believe in the PIE model for career success? I disagree; however, this is how it works.

30. How often do you exercise? Once per month

31. How much time do you take off each year to recharge your batteries? Two times per year for seven days

32. May I use your name in the book? Keep confidential.

33. Whom would you recommend I interview for this book?

34. How would you characterize yourself (either introverted or extroverted)? Introverted

35. What introverted or extroverted qualities do you daily display to the general public?

    Introverted behaviors—I keep to myself. I show up alone and respect others' space.

36. On a scale of one to ten, with ten being easiest, how easy is it for you to start a conversation with a stranger? Nine

37. On a scale of one to ten, with ten being easiest, how easy is it for you to network with others in the workplace? Seven

38. What are some tools you use to maintain relationships with others? Communications, knowledge, email, texting

39. What is your preferred method of communication (email, in person, phone, and so forth)? Email. I like documentation.

40. How much energy does it take for you to navigate the corporate or white-collar working environment? It take a lot of energy. I don't know what to expect. The rules can change. It's important keep your guard up.

Emotional Intelligence and Introversion/Extroversion Tendency Interview (40 Questions)

Send to Dr. Reginald Ramsey, PhD, MBA, CISA, @ <u>HRTC1906@ gmail.com</u>

Name:___Black/Female/Professional _____

Response Date: __5/8/2022_____

1. What is your official job title? Cashier

2. How long have you been in your current role? Sixteen years

3. What attributes or skills helped you to reach your current career level? Customer service, personal relationships

4. What does your typical day entail? Please elaborate as much as possible. I relate to people. I ring up sales, prepare the store for customers, inspect the inventory, and ensure the needs of customers are met.

5. How many hours do you work per week? Thirty-four to thirty-six

6. What advice would you give to someone who wants to be in your position someday? Get experience.

7. What has been the role of mentors or coaches in your career advancement? None

8. How many mentors do you have or have had over your career? None

9. How often do you speak or communicate with your mentor or mentors? NA

10. How do you balance your work with your private life? I work only four days per week.

11. How often do you set goals? I didn't set goals.

12. What type of goals do you set (yearly, monthly, and so forth)? NA

13. How long have you been working in the market space? Since I was sixteen or thirty-seven years

14. What was your first job? I worked at a local hospital.

15. What valuable lessons have you learned over your career? If you want more, you must do more.

16. What type of spiritual life do you have? I believe in God.

17. Do you attend or engage in any religious activities? Yes

18. What role has emotional intelligence played in your career progression? It has done a lot in my career.

19. What are some unwritten rules or norms you learned from being in a white-collar environment? Your manager can set the tone of the workplace or work environment; this tone affects the employees.

20. Did your parents or grandparents work in a white-collar setting? Yes or no? No

21. Did your parents or grandparents teach you how to navigate a white-collar working environment? No

22. What did your parents or grandparents teach you about working in a white-collar environment? Nothing

23. How did you learn about these unwritten rules or norms (observation, mentors, mistakes)? Experience

24. Currently, how many individuals do you mentor? Three

25. How often do you listen to or read about successful individuals? Rarely

26. What role has self-talk played in your career success? A major part

27. How do you motivate yourself each day? I listen to motivational speakers.

28. What are some of your hobbies? Walking, exercising, shopping, listening to music, listening to comedy

29. Do you believe in the PIE model for career success? Yes

30. How often do you exercise? Four to five days per week

31. How much time do you take off each year to recharge your batteries? As often as I can

32. May I use your name in the book? Keep confidential.

33. Whom would you recommend I interview for this book? NA

34. How would you characterize yourself (either introverted or extroverted)? Both

35. What introverted or extroverted qualities do you daily display to the general public?

    Extroverted—I'm friendly to people; I like to learn from other people.

Introverted—I enjoy time alone to reflect and come with some ideas.

36. On a scale of one to ten, with ten being easiest, how easy is it for you to start a conversation with a stranger? Ten

37. On a scale of one to ten, with ten being easiest, how easy is it for you to network with others in the workplace? Ten

38. What are some tools you use to maintain relationships with others? Communication, phone, text, in person

39. What is your preferred method of communication (email, in person, phone, and so forth)? Phone

40. How much energy does it take for you to navigate the corporate or white-collar working environment? Not much energy

Emotional Intelligence and Introversion/Extroversion Tendency Interview (40 Questions)

Send to Dr. Reginald Ramsey, PhD, MBA, CISA, @ HRTC1906@gmail.com

Name:___Black/Female/Professional_____

Response Date: ___5/5/2022_____

1. What is your official job title? LPN

2. How long have you been in your current role? Fourteen years

3. What attributes or skills helped you to reach your current career level? Hard work, certification, effective communication, ability

to multitask. I love what I do. I love people. The job is not for the faint of heart.

4. What does your typical day entail? Please elaborate much as possible. It is very detail oriented. I communicate and listen to the patients and family members. I need to be able to be a critical thinker and follow up.

5. How many hours do you work per week? At least sixty (five times twelve)

6. What advice would you give to someone who wants to be in your position someday? Don't do it just for the money.

7. What has been the role of mentors or coaches in your career advancement? I had people coach me on better attitudes toward things, including not being on the defensive.

8. How many mentors do you have or have had over your career? No real mentors

9. How often do you speak or communicate with your mentor or mentors? NA

10. How do you balance your work with your private life? No balance

11. How often do you set goals? I don't set a lot of goals.

12. What type of goals do you set (yearly, monthly, and so forth)? My goal is to be sixty-five years old and not have to work.

13. How long have you been working in the market space? Approximately twenty-one years

14. What was your first job? Spousal abuse center

15. What valuable lessons have you learned over your career? Nobody is your friend in the workplace.

16. What type of spiritual life do you have? I am spiritual.

17. Do you attend or engage in any religious activities? Not currently

18. What role has emotional intelligence played in your career progression? It has helped to become wiser and taught me how to understand others.

19. What are some unwritten rules or norms you learned from being in a white-collar environment? There is a double standard. Angry black women are rude and aggressive. This is accepted by other races.

20. Did your parents or grandparents work in a white-collar setting? Yes or no? Yes

21. Did your parents or grandparents teach you how to navigate a white-collar working environment? No

22. What did your parents or grandparents teach you about working in a white-collar environment? Nothing

23. How did you learn about these unwritten rules or norms (observation, mentors, mistakes)? Through mistakes and personal experience

24. Currently, how many individuals do you mentor? None

25. How often do you listen to or read about successful individuals? Not a lot

26. What role has self-talk played in your career success? It helped me to get where I am now.

27. How do you motivate yourself each day? Prayer

28. What are some of your hobbies? Shopping, traveling, sleeping

29. Do you believe in the PIE model for career success? This is the first time I'm hearing about it.

30. How often do you exercise? I don't.

31. How much time do you take off each year to recharge your batteries? Once or twice per year

32. May I use your name in the book? No

33. Whom would you recommend I interview for this book? NA

34. How would you characterize yourself (either introverted or extroverted)? Both

35. What introverted or extroverted qualities do you daily display to the general public? I'm extroverted like energized around people; people are excited to see me.

36. On a scale of one to ten, with ten being easiest, how easy is it for you to start a conversation with a stranger? Ten

37. On a scale of one to ten, with ten being easiest, how easy is it for you to network with others in the workplace? Seven

38. What are some tools you use to maintain relationships with others? I keep in touch by phone.

39. What is your preferred method of communication (email, in person, phone, and so forth)? Phone

40. How much energy does it take for you to navigate the corporate or white-collar working environment? Not a lot of energy

CHAPTER 5

SURVEY RESPONSES: WHITE-COLLAR PROFESSIONALS

Emotional Intelligence and Introversion/Extroversion Tendency Interview (40 Questions)

Send to Dr. Reginald Ramsey, PhD, MBA, CISA, @ HRTC1906@ gmail.com

Name:____Black/Male/Professional_____

Response Date: _____July 5, 2022_____

1. What is your official job title? Attorney

2. How long have you been in your current role? Fifteen years

3. What attributes or skills helped you to reach your current career level? Determination, perseverance. I read a lot (articles in the *New York Times*, Washington Post). I'm open minded.

4. What does your typical day entail? Please elaborate as much as possible. I did everything. I chased criminals, hoped for crime.

5. How many hours do you work per week? More than forty: sixty to eighty

6. What advice would you give to someone who wants to be in your position someday? Be observant, drop your ego, learn from others, and talk to law students. It's a journey.

7. What has been the role of mentors or coaches in your career advancement? They had knowledge. I talked to them; they had a wealth of information. Add your favor to it; learn from them and watch them.

8. How many mentors do you have or have had over your career? I started at church; I had hundreds of mentors.

9. How often do you speak or communicate with your mentor or mentors? As often as possible. I observed a lot; I didn't talk a lot.

10. How do you balance your work or life? I burned both sides of the candle.

11. How often do you set goals? I set monthly goals; the exit plan is quarterly.

12. What type of goals do you set (yearly, monthly, and so forth)? Long and quarterly

13. How long have you been working in the market space? Fifteen years

14. What was your first job? State legislatures caucus for two years, then law school

15. What valuable lessons have you learned over your career? You've got to be honest, honest with yourself; be focused and flexible.

16. What type of spiritual life do you have? I'm very spiritual; my family were church members.

17. Do you attend or engage in any religious activities?

18. What role has emotional intelligence played in your career progression? I learned to be patient, stay cool, be mindful, and meditate.

19. What are some unwritten rules or norms you learned from being in a white-collar environment? Make friends with your enemies; play both sides. Be careful what you see. You've gotta work three times as hard.

20. Did your parents or grandparents work in a white-collar setting? Yes or no? No

21. Did your parents or grandparents teach you how to navigate a white-collar working environment? No. I was put in private schools; my parents attended major schools.

22. What did your parents or grandparents teach you about working in a white-collar environment? Put the work in; sacrifice but keep your identity.

23. How did you learn about these unwritten rules or norms (observation, mentors, mistakes)? Mentors and observation

24. Currently, how many individuals do you mentor? Zero

25. How often do you listen to or read about successful individuals? Every day. I like the library.

26. What role has self-talk played in your career success? It helped me to navigate the rules and execute the game.

27. How do you motivate yourself each day? I think about my ancestors and have gratitude. I show the world.

28. What are some of your hobbies? Golf

29. Do you believe in the PIE model for career success? I believe it.

30. How often do you exercise? Daily (two times)

31. How much time do you take off each year to recharge your batteries? Quarterly

32. May I use your name in the book? Keep confidential.

33. Whom would you recommend I interview for this book?

34. How would you characterize yourself (either introverted or extroverted)? Introverted

35. What introverted or extroverted qualities do you daily display to the general public?

    Introverted—I like jazz music and make observations.

36. On a scale of one to ten, with ten being easiest, how easy is it for you to start a conversation with a stranger? Eight to nine

37. On a scale of one to ten, with ten being easiest, how easy is it for you to network with others in the workplace? Ten

38. What are some tools you use to maintain relationships with others? Observe others; be worldly.

39. What is your preferred method of communication (email, in person, phone, and so forth)? All of the above

40. How much energy does it take for you to navigate the corporate or white-collar working environment? I takes a lot.

Emotional Intelligence and Introversion/Extroversion Tendency Interview (40 Questions)

Send to Dr. Reginald Ramsey, PhD, MBA, CISA, @ <u>HRTC1906@gmail.com</u>

Name: Black/Female/Professional_____ _____

Response Date: _____07/24/2022_____

1. What is your official job title? Project manager/program manager, IT Transformation and Consolidation

2. How long have you been in your current role? Four years

3. What attributes or skills helped you to reach your current career level?

   Communicating (verbal and nonverbal) with people from different levels of the organization; status reporting; hosting and presenting in meetings; problem-solving; having the ability to coach, train, and lead others; possessing business and technical acumen

4. What does your typical day entail? Please elaborate as much as possible.

   Scheduling and hosting meetings, scheduling projects, managing project budget, minimizing risk and issues across the IT Transformation and Consolidation program, managing eight IT infrastructure project teams and task activities, writing status reports, communicating status to steering committee and project teams, presenting to group chief information officers once a year

5. How many hours do you work per week? Forty. Occasionally I work over forty, but I try to have a good work and life balance.

6. What advice would you give to someone who wants to be in your position someday?

    Take Toastmaster classes, train on effective communication, and work on managing conflict. Improve writing skills; always be succinct and clear when communicating. Learn to have constructive crucial conversations, set boundaries and expectations when presenting during meetings, keep status and meeting with senior leadership at best thirty minutes minimum. Be prepared for questions from peers and leaders at the drop of a dime. If you don't know something, say, "I do not know, but give me X time, and I will get back to you with an answer." Show leadership by being an example of what you like to see in a leader. Strengthen your spiritual life, get rest, eat right, and exercise. Always be aware of what is going on in your environment.

7. What has been the role of mentors or coaches in your career advancement?

    The roles of mentors and coaches in my life have been procurement manager, pastor, sisters in Christ, professors from school, IT managers, chief information officers, system analysts, my immediate supervisors, project managers, program managers, and family.

8. How many mentors do you have or have had over your career? Early in my career, I had up to twenty. Now I would say I have about twelve people keep in contact with.

9. How often do you speak or communicate with your mentor or mentors? I try to speak with anyone on a weekly basis based on my needs. I keep a journal on whom I work with and what the goal of the meeting will be. I detail what my accomplishments are. I role-play with my mentor any situation I had trouble with

and identify any lessons learned and plans for next week to meet my goal or goals.

10. How do you balance your work with your private life? I make sure I address my capacity to work on additional project loads with my manager and keep my work hours at forty per week. I take time to sit still and be quiet, relax, enjoy time with my family, and do something positive and different each week. I make sure I work on my spiritual and physical well-being.

11. How often do you set goals?

I set goals daily at round 6 a.m.

12. What type of goals do you set (yearly, monthly, and so forth)?

I have work goals for the day and family goals like visiting relatives, taking family trips, working in the garden, and so forth. My spiritual goal is to listen to Christian music or scripture for twenty minutes a day.

13. How long have you been working in the market space?

Thirty years

14. What was your first job?

My first job ever was working at McDonald's at age fifteen.

15. What valuable lessons have you learned over your career?

Never give up. Give yourself grace for the things you do not know, learn as much as you can about your profession, and know you and your boundaries and expectations in the workplace. Be professional at all times, even when you do not want to. Be willing to coach and mentor others.

16. What type of spiritual life do you have? Christian faith. Jesus Christ is my personal Savior.

17. Do you attend or engage in any religious activities? Sometimes

18. What role has emotional intelligence played in your career progression?

    Emotional intelligence plays a great part in my career profession. I have the ability to manage my emotions in a positive way in any situation at work. To do my job effectively, I need to understand business needs, communication vehicles to use, and how teams work to effectively manage my projects and be a servant to the team. I provide team members with feedback, I receive feedback from my management and peers, and I work through difficult and challenging relationships at work.

19. What are some unwritten rules or norms you learned from being in a white-collar environment?

    I have learned not to give so much of myself to the point that I can get sick or die from doing my job. The company will only replace you with another Charlita.

20. Did your parents or grandparents work in a white-collar setting? Yes or no?

    No

21. Did your parents or grandparents teach you how to navigate a white-collar working environment? No

22. What did your parents or grandparents teach you about working in a white-collar environment?

My parent only taught me to respect myself and make sure they paid me for my work.

23. How did you learn about these unwritten rules or norms (observation, mentors, mistakes)?

I learned through personal experiences.

24. Currently, how many individuals do you mentor?

Ten

25. How often do you listen to or read about successful individuals?
Weekly

26. What role has self-talk played in your career success?

It plays a big role in my career and on Sunday afternoon. Sometimes I have anxiety because I know there are eight projects to manage, and these are large projects. I do positive self-talk in my mind to quiet my spirit and stress. I reassure myself that I can do only the best I can. There is no need to worry. I need to let tomorrow take care of itself. The anxiety is gone by the morning. Then I am rocking and rolling.

27. How do you motivate yourself each day?

I rise at 4:30 a.m. before the family gets up and put on Christian music or review a verse in the Bible. I say a short prayer, start housecleaning or work out, then prepare for work. From 7:30 a.m. to 8 a.m., I have a great cup of coffee my husband prepares for me. I sit and enjoy life until it is time to go to work.

28. What are some of your hobbies?

Gardening, interior design, watching movies

29. Do you believe in the PIE model for career success?

    I have not heard of it.

30. How often do you exercise? Two days a week

31. How much time do you take off each year to recharge your batteries? I take one week of vacation a year.

32. May I use your name in the book?

    Yes

33. Whom would you recommend I interview for this book?

    I would say individuals who report to senior leadership and those in leadership roles.

34. How would you characterize yourself (either introverted or extroverted)?

    I am an introverted thinker and extroverted communicator.

35. What introverted or extroverted qualities do you daily display to the general public?

    Based on feedback from people I work with, I would say my qualities of being introverted are the following: being self-aware, shy, analytical, and detailed; having insight into others' behavior; and being tired after working with so many people in a day. I have few friends but are very close to them.

    Extrovert qualities include written presentations, the ability to communicate with large groups of individuals, and the ability to keep people engaged in meetings. I keep teams energized and motivated to meet work goals.

36. On a scale of one to ten, with ten being easiest, how easy is it for you to start a conversation with a stranger? Ten

37. On a scale of one to ten, with ten being easiest, how easy is it for you to network with others in the workplace?

    Eight

38. What are some tools you use to maintain relationships with others?

    Have a good, healthy self-care regimen. Set good boundaries. Learn to say no. Be honest to people. Know yourself and always have good intentions toward others. Listen to their feedback. I am always present emotionally and physically, even via LinkedIn, Facebook, texts, Zoom, or phone calls.

39. What is your preferred method of communication (email, in person, phone, and so forth)?

    Phone or Webex calls

40. How much energy does it take for you to navigate the corporate or white-collar working environment?

41. It takes a lot of energy. The higher up the ladder in corporate environment, the more politics, and the more important it is that you have information and facts to share at a moment's notice and know when to be quiet and when to drive a discussion. I have had to make a lot of decisions and present them to leadership to get their blessing to move forward with the decisions I proposed. This works for me to get results the rest of the organization needs to do what it need to do.

Emotional Intelligence and Introversion/Extroversion Tendency Interview (40 Questions)

Send to Dr. Reginald Ramsey, PhD, MBA, CISA, @ <u>HRTC1906@</u> <u>gmail.com</u>

Name:___Black/Female/Professional_____

Response Date: ___July 17, 2022_____

1. What is your official job title? Claim insurance generalist

2. How long have you been in your current role? One year

3. What attributes or skills helped you to reach your current career level? Verbal and written communications skills, passing state license exams and insurance exams

4. What does your typical day entail? Please elaborate as much as possible. Investigating accidents, negotiating bodies claims

5. How many hours do you work per week? Fifty

6. What advice would you give to someone who wants to be in your position someday? Enhance communications skills, writing skills, and writing legal documents. Use your written skills. Develop good reading skills, math skills, communication skills, and negotiation skills. Develop empathy. Don't overspeak to people. Use great communications with great English. Don't split verbs. I get assigned to her.

7. What has been the role of mentors or coaches in your career advancement? I was asked to mentor others by the company; mentors help her to grow. She learned a lot; she took notes from the mentors. She learned how to follow up with others.

8. How many mentors do you have or have had over your career? Ten

9. How often do you speak or communicate with your mentor or mentors? It is on a situational basis, on average two times per month.

10. How do you balance your work with your private life? Start on time without distractions or cell phones. Stay focused on scheduled activities, to-do lists, and emails.

11. How often do you set goals? Daily. I write down an idea and see the goal written down. This helps me to stay focused. I learned this technique from college and high school. Dream something and write down your goal. My parents helped me. They said, "You can do whatever you want to do." My teachers and parents helped me.

12. What type of goals do you set (yearly, monthly, and so forth)? Daily

13. How long have you been working in the market space? Thirty-six years

14. What was your first job? Clerk

15. What valuable lessons have you learned over your career?

16. What type of spiritual life do you have? I have a great spiritual life. I daily start with prayer. This helps to sustain my marriage.

17. Do you attend or engage in any religious activities? Yes

18. What role has emotional intelligence played in your career progression? It is very important. I acknowledge my peers; that's a great point. "I agree with X." Don't let other people know your

feelings; don't project a negative attitude. Learn how to manage your emotions.

19. What are some unwritten rules or norms you learned from being in a white-collar environment? Know your audience.

20. Did your parents or grandparents work in a white-collar setting? Yes or no? No

21. Did your parents or grandparents teach you how to navigate a white-collar working environment? No

22. What did your parents or grandparents teach you about working in a white-collar environment? Do your best.

23. How did you learn about these unwritten rules or norms (observation, mentors, mistakes)? All of the above

24. Currently, how many individuals do you mentor? One

25. How often do you listen to or read about successful individuals? Infrequently

26. What role has self-talk played in your career success? It is important to me; I can do all things through Christ.

27. How do you motivate yourself each day? I think about the task. I dream.

28. What are some of your hobbies? Cooking, baking, gardening, sewing, doing home design, conducting home improvement

29. Do you believe in the PIE model for career success? Wholeheartedly I agree with this concept. I believe in associating with people above your level; they will inspire you. Don't let others drag you down. Be willing to go out of your comfort zone.

30. How often do you exercise? Not enough

31. How much time do you take off each year to recharge your batteries? A week

32. May I use your name in the book? Keep confidential.

33. Whom would you recommend I interview for this book?

34. How would you characterize yourself (either introverted or extroverted)? Extroverted

35. What introverted or extroverted qualities do you daily display to the general public?

    Extroverted—I don't meet any strangers. I have a pleasant attitude and smile. I invite a smile.

36. On a scale of one to ten, with ten being easiest, how easy is it for you to start a conversation with a stranger? Ten

37. On a scale of one to ten, with ten being easiest, how easy is it for you to network with others in the workplace? Ten

38. What are some tools you use to maintain relationships with others? Excel at name recognition. Remember people's names. Have a pleasant attitude and knowledge of the conversation.

39. What is your preferred method of communication (email, in person, phone, and so forth)? Phone

40. How much energy does it take for you to navigate the corporate or white-collar working environment? It takes a lot of energy.

Emotional Intelligence and Introversion/Extroversion Tendency Interview (40 Questions)

Send to Dr. Reginald Ramsey, PhD, MBA, CISA, @ HRTC1906@ gmail.com

Name:__Black/Female/Professional_____

Response Date: ___July 8, 2022_____

1. What is your official job title? Property manager

2. How long have you been in your current role? Twenty-five years

3. What attributes or skills helped you to reach your current career level? A love of being with people, being able to communicate with the public. I've got a business background with apartment management and a legal background. I understand the law.

4. What does your typical day entail? Please elaborate as much as possible. Monitoring the day-to-day property, collecting money, serving in property management, being an office manager, serving as a social worker, being a ground worker, primarily maintaining the property and collection of money

5. How many hours do you work per week? Forty to fifty hours

6. What advice would you give to someone who wants to be in your position someday? It's not for everybody. You need to work with the public and can't be a shy person. You will need to speak with investors and owners. You've got to love working with the public. Working with housing is different; senior citizens have a sense of entitlement. It's a different type of work.

7. What has been the role of mentors or coaches in your career advancement? I didn't have a lot of mentors or coaches; I have

been the mentor and coach. I did have one person as a "go to" who coached me.

8. How many mentors do you have or have had over your career? Limited

9. How often do you speak or communicate with your mentor or mentors? Limited

10. How do you balance your work with your private life? I keep them separate; it's difficult. I like going to concerts, shopping, and going out to eat.

11. How often do you set goals? Annually, quarterly, and monthly. It depends.

12. What type of goals do you set (yearly, monthly, and so forth)? I set financial goals as well as project goals, spiritual goals, and family goals. I reevaluate and reassess my goals.

13. How long have you been working in the market space? Since thirteenth year

14. What was your first job? Fast-food restaurant

15. What valuable lessons have you learned over your career? Integrity and self-respect are important. Keep your word. Be a decent person. Documentation is big. Be a person of character. Be real. Be yourself.

16. What type of spiritual life do you have? I have a personal relationship with the Lord, but it isn't the type of spiritual life I would like to have; I love the Lord.

17. Do you attend or engage in any religious activities? I attend regular church.

18. What role has emotional intelligence played in your career progression? During the pandemic, we lost forty residents; I had to comfort the families. I had to deal with my staff regarding disagreements and conflict resolution. I had to be sensitive to both parties and evaluate the situation. I can be vulnerable.

19. What are some unwritten rules or norms you learned from being in a white-collar environment? Don't fraternize with the residents or contractors. Do things by the book.

20. Did your parents or grandparents work in a white-collar setting? Yes or no? No

21. Did your parents or grandparents teach you how to navigate a white-collar working environment? No

22. What did your parents or grandparents teach you about working in a white-collar environment? NA

23. How did you learn about these unwritten rules or norms (observation, mentors, mistakes)? Mistakes, experience

24. Currently, how many individuals do you mentor? None officially. I am in a support group of eight women; we support each other.

25. How often do you listen to or read about successful individuals? Daily. I listen to the news; I read every day.

26. What role has self-talk played in your career success? It plays a different role. It was more strict. It is more difficult now; it pushes me. I am working on my discipline. I take care of

27. How do you motivate yourself each day? It's rough; it starts at night. I have to be prepared. I have devotions in the morning and encourage myself with affirmations and prayers.

28. What are some of your hobbies? Skating, music, concerts, stages, going to museums, shopping, reading, doing nothing. I love to clean up.

29. Do you believe in the PIE model for career success? I agree in various settings.

30. How often do you exercise? Four times per week

31. How much time do you take off each year to recharge your batteries? Four weeks, one week per quarter

32. May I use your name in the book? Keep confidential.

33. Whom would you recommend I interview for this book?

34. How would you characterize yourself (either introverted or extroverted)? Extroverted

35. What introverted or extroverted qualities do you daily display to the general public?

    Extroverted—I'm a loud, colorful, and good person. I love people.

36. On a scale of one to ten, with ten being easiest, how easy is it for you to start a conversation with a stranger? Ten

37. On a scale of one to ten, with ten being easiest, how easy is it for you to network with others in the workplace? Ten

38. What are some tools you use to maintain relationships with others? I use constant communication through text and phone. I call them.

39. What is your preferred method of communication (email, in person, phone, and so forth)? In person, on the phone, text, or email

40. How much energy does it take for you to navigate the corporate or white-collar working environment? It depends on the day or situation. As the only black woman, I have to show my work ethic; I have to constantly prove myself.

Emotional Intelligence and Introversion/Extroversion Tendency Interview (40 Questions)

Send to Dr. Reginald Ramsey, PhD, MBA, CISA, @ <u>HRTC1906@gmail.com</u>

Name:___Female/White/Professional _____

Response Date: _____6/3/2022_____

1. What is your official job title? Consultant, security architect

2. How long have you been in your current role? Ten years

3. What attributes or skills helped you to reach your current career level? Interest in the area, passion for the topic. I am interested in questions and challenges; I like learning new things. Security was new; I asked questions, wanting to make things better. It was hard work.

4. What does your typical day entail? Please elaborate as much as possible. There is no "typical" day; days never go as expected. I should have had a strategic role; I had to deal with emergency situations, emails, and meetings.

5. How many hours do you work per week? They varied. I'm a working mom. Sometimes I worked sixty-plus hours per week.

6. What advice would you give to someone who wants to be in your position someday? Network, talk to other people, ask other people questions, and be willing to learn new things.

7. What has been the role of mentors or coaches in your career advancement? Early on I didn't use them; I learned the hard way. I had a mentor later in my career; I had to humble myself and ask for help.

8. How many mentors do you have or have had over your career? More mentees; I had about a half dozen toward the second half of my career.

9. How often do you speak or communicate with your mentor or mentors? It depends on the mentor. Many meetings were monthly over lunch on a regular basis.

10. How do you balance your work or life? It takes a lot of juggling, prioritizing, and organizing. I did a lot for my kids; I worked from home.

11. How often do you set goals? Frequently. I use a to-do list (now); on a long-term basis, I don't do this as often.

12. What type of goals do you set (yearly, monthly, and so forth)? Mostly weekly; some are monthly. Some are long term.

13. How long have you been working in the market space? Forty-five years

14. What was your first job? Computer science department in college

15. What valuable lessons have you learned over your career? Figure out how to fit in different environments; modify your message as needed for your audience. The Serenity Prayer: accept the things

that can't be changed, change the things you can, and have the wisdom to understand the difference.

16. What type of spiritual life do you have? I'm very spiritual but not religious. I respect people. I have strong ethics.

17. Do you attend or engage in any religious activities? I used to; it became too judgmental.

18. What role has emotional intelligence played in your career progression? It is very important. It helps to work with others. It helps to have empathy.

19. What are some unwritten rules or norms you learned from being in a white-collar environment? Stay away from politics. Dress for success. Take care in how you express new ideas. Don't take the last cup of coffee. Learn how to fit in your environment while still being you.

20. Did your parents or grandparents work in a white-collar setting? Yes or no? No

21. Did your parents or grandparents teach you how to navigate a white-collar working environment? No

22. What did your parents or grandparents teach you about working in a white-collar environment? They insisted on education. Hard work and personal ethics are important; this is true for any job.

23. How did you learn about these unwritten rules or norms (observation, mentors, mistakes)? All of the above!

24. Currently, how many individuals do you mentor? Two

25. How often do you listen to or read about successful individuals? Periodically; it's always interesting to see what traits helped others

succeed. Sometimes it was just being in the right place at the right time and being smart enough to recognize that.

26. What role has self-talk played in your career success? A lot. Sometimes it was hard to keep the self-talk positive. Too much negative self-talk can be damaging, but you also need to be realistic and understand when you make a mistake and learn from it.

27. How do you motivate yourself each day? I try to go into each day with gratitude, regardless of the circumstances. I try to do the "right thing"; the right words matter for motivation.

28. What are some of your hobbies? Walking, yoga, reading, volunteering

29. Do you believe in the PIE model for career success? I do. Performance and image were never a problem; exposure was. Mentoring can help with exposure.

30. How often do you exercise? Usually two to three times per week

31. How much time do you take off each year to recharge your batteries? Not enough

32. May I use your name in the book? Keep confidential.

33. Whom would you recommend I interview for this book?

34. How would you characterize yourself (either introverted or extroverted)? I'm somewhat introverted but not shy; I enjoy people in smaller groups or one on one.

35. What introverted or extroverted qualities do you daily display to the general public? I'm polite but not outspoken. I think before I answer a question. This has been interpreted as "always wanting

to be right," but I don't answer—or I answer, "I don't know" to something I have no clue about. I won't "force" myself into a conversation; I'm confident but not showy.

36. On a scale of one to ten, with ten being easiest, how easy is it for you to start a conversation with a stranger? It depends on the situation, but seven to eight; it helps if I have a lead-in (e.g., "What a cute dog" or "Love your jacket. Where did you get it?")

37. On a scale of one to ten, with ten being easiest, how easy is it for you to network with others in the workplace? Eight to nine. In the workplace, it's easier because you probably know the individual and have common goals.

38. What are some tools you use to maintain relationships with others? Social media (LinkedIn, Facebook, Instagram), individual messages, texts, regular Zoom meetings with family, phone calls with family and close friends, meals, impromptu porch parties with friends and neighbors

39. What is your preferred method of communication (email, in person, phone, and so forth)? It depends on the person and the context. For day-to-day stuff, I use texts or other messaging platforms. I use email for things I want to memorialize and do in-person meetings for sensitive conversations.

40. How much energy does it take for you to navigate the corporate or white-collar working environment? Sometimes a lot! To work a project or get an idea considered, you have to know who to talk to, how to get his or her interest, how to get his or her support, and so forth. This is where good mentors can come in.

Emotional Intelligence and Introversion/Extroversion Tendency Interview (40 Questions)

Send to Dr. Reginald Ramsey, PhD, MBA, CISA, @ HRTC1906@gmail.com

Name:___Female/Black/Professional_____

Response Date: _____5/28/2022_____

1. What is your official job title? Health systems specialist

2. How long have you been in your current role? Since 2013

3. What attributes or skills helped you to reach your current career level? Education, effective oral and written communication, being assertive, being an expert in a field; having experience and training, and being persistent and resilient. Know the players. Be an expert in your trade or field.

4. What does your typical day entail? Please elaborate as much as possible. I research policies, provide guidance to health care providers, respond to emails, and attend three meetings per day.

5. How many hours do you work per week? Four or five

6. What advice would you give to someone who wants to be in your position someday? Have self-confidence. Be independent. Be a self-starter and decision maker. Develop communication skills and don't second-guess yourself.

7. What has been the role of mentors or coaches in your career advancement? Mentors helped me to stop second-guessing myself. Be okay if you are not right on the mark. Don't be afraid to fail. Make decisions. Get comfortable with failure. Don't be

afraid to say, "I don't know." Be a good problem solver. Identify gaps for various policies; give leaders the picture they can't see.

8. How many mentors do you have or have had over your career? Four

9. How often do you speak or communicate with your mentor or mentors? Daily

10. How do you balance your work or life? Set some professional boundaries; family comes first. Don't call during vacations. Create "white space" on your calendar.

11. How often do you set goals? Weekly

12. What type of goals do you set (yearly, monthly, and so forth)? Weekly

13. How long have you been working in the market space? Twenty-five years

14. What was your first job? McDonald's at age nineteen

15. What valuable lessons have you learned over your career? Remind in a professional mode, even when off duty. Don't mix business and pleasure.

16. What type of spiritual life do you have? I pray daily. I listen to *Our Daily Bread*. I stretch.

17. Do you attend or engage in any religious activities? Yes

18. What role has emotional intelligence played in your career progression? It has helped me to navigate toward promotions, read a room, listen to others, and express empathy. I have learned when to give grace versus holding to the fire. Words are important.

19. What are some unwritten rules or norms you learned from being in a white-collar environment? Your rules are different; expectations are different. Saying less is much better.

20. Did your parents or grandparents work in a white-collar setting? Yes or no? My mother did.

21. Did your parents or grandparents teach you how to navigate a white-collar working environment?

22. What did your parents or grandparents teach you about working in a white-collar environment? Work harder. Stand up for yourself. Address microaggressions.

23. How did you learn about these unwritten rules or norms (observation, mentors, mistakes)? All of the above and mom and grandmother. Listen to family members.

24. Currently, how many individuals do you mentor? Too many to count. I have young mentors and older individuals. I give advice to many people.

25. How often do you listen to or read about successful individuals? Daily

26. What role has self-talk played in your career success? It has given me self-confidence and growth in emotional intelligence. I know I belong.

27. How do you motivate yourself each day? I think about all I can have if I make more money or revenue. I think about my future.

28. What are some of your hobbies? Reading, medical research, different planets, cooking, traveling, and walking

29. Do you believe in the PIE model for career success? Yes, because performance is important. How people perceive me is important too. People need to connect with me.

30. How often do you exercise? Three times per week; it is rigorous.

31. How much time do you take off each year to recharge your batteries? Four weeks per year

32. May I use your name in the book? Keep confidential.

33. Whom would you recommend I interview for this book? NA

34. How would you characterize yourself (either introverted or extroverted)? Introverted

35. What introverted or extroverted qualities do you daily display to the general public?

    I take all the information in before I speak; I think before I speak. I'm not the loudest or most talkative person. I speak when I need to.

36. On a scale of one to ten, with ten being easiest, how easy is it for you to start a conversation with a stranger? Ten

37. On a scale of one to ten, with ten being easiest, how easy is it for you to network with others in the workplace? Ten

38. What are some tools you use to maintain relationships with others? I reach out to them. I send an email and say, "Let's connect." I connect with people; I block out time to connect with people.

39. What is your preferred method of communication (email, in person, phone, and so forth)? Email, phone would like

40. How much energy does it take for you to navigate the corporate or white-collar working environment? Not as much as it used to be. I knew the games and politics; it was exhausting as a black female. I spent two hours trying to play by the rules.

Emotional Intelligence and Introversion/Extroversion Tendency Interview (40 Questions)

Send to Dr. Reginald Ramsey, PhD, MBA, CISA, @ HRTC1906@ gmail.com

Name:___Black/Male/Professional_____

Response Date: _____7/23/2022_____

1. What is your official job title? Associate director

2. How long have you been in your current role? Three years

3. What attributes or skills helped you to reach your current career level? A technical background, communication skills, high emotional intelligence skills, presentation skills, listening skills, and facilitation skills. I was able to navigate the complexity of corporate America.

4. What does your typical day entail? Please elaborate as much as possible. Having meetings, planning sessions, thinking, collaborating with others, developing ideas, mentoring, coaching, getting mentored and coached, planning, executing a plan, updating management and leaders, doing thought leadership

5. How many hours do you work per week? Forty to fifty

6. What advice would you give to someone who wants to be in your position someday? Go for it; don't be afraid to fail. Learn from your mistakes. Get up after you fail and keep pushing forward.

7. What has been the role of mentors or coaches in your career advancement? Mentors and coaches have helped me to navigate the corporate environment with more confidence.

8. How many mentors do you have or have had over your career? Over one hundred

9. How often do you speak or communicate with your mentor or mentors? Some on a weekly basis, a monthly basis, or a quarterly basis

10. How do you balance your work with your private life? I enjoy "alone or me time." I am able to work remotely for a week per month. This allows me to focus and reset my goals and priorities.

11. How often do you set goals? Daily, monthly, quarterly, annually, every five years, and every ten years

12. What type of goals do you set (yearly, monthly, and so forth)? Daily, monthly, quarterly, annually, every five years, and every ten years

13. How long have you been working in the market space? Since 1984 or thirty-eight years

14. What was your first job? Working for a large grocery chain. I took groceries to people's cars in the hot Texas weather.

15. What valuable lessons have you learned over your career? Never quit. Keep learning. Develop a love of books and personal growth. Stay coachable. Actively listen.

16. What type of spiritual life do you have? I have a very active and real spiritual life. I have morning devotions and daily prayer. I usually fast and pray weekly. This helps to center me spiritually and emotionally.

17. Do you attend or engage in any religious activities? Yes

18. What role has emotional intelligence played in your career progression? Emotional intelligence has helped me to understand

myself. Emotional intelligence helps me to empathize with various people. It helps to keep me motivated daily. It helps me to socialize and engage with others.

19. What are some unwritten rules or norms you learned from being in a white-collar environment? Get to know the players by asking for help. Don't make assumptions based on your life experiences. Appearance matters.

20. Did your parents or grandparents work in a white-collar setting? Yes or no? No

21. Did your parents or grandparents teach you how to navigate a white-collar working environment? No

22. What did your parents or grandparents teach you about working in a white-collar environment? Work hard, and people will reward you.

23. How did you learn about these unwritten rules or norms (observation, mentors, mistakes)? Mistakes, mentors, and observation

24. Currently, how many individuals do you mentor? Twelve to fifteen

25. How often do you listen to or read about successful individuals? Daily

26. What role has self-talk played in your career success? It helps to motivate me in the mornings. It keeps me going forward.

27. How do you motivate yourself each day? Self-talk and goals

28. What are some of your hobbies? Chess, golf, tennis, reading, traveling, writing

29. Do you believe in the PIE model for career success? Yes

30. How often do you exercise? Daily

31. How much time do you take off each year to recharge your batteries? Four weeks

32. May I use your name in the book? Keep confidential.

33. Whom would you recommend I interview for this book? NA

34. How would you characterize yourself (either introverted or extroverted)? Introverted

35. What introverted or extroverted qualities do you daily display to the general public?

    I enjoy one-on-one interactions with others. I enjoy meeting new and interesting people. I enjoy learning and growing. I enjoy writing and playing chess.

36. On a scale of one to ten, with ten being easiest, how easy is it for you to start a conversation with a stranger? Seven

37. On a scale of one to ten, with ten being easiest, how easy is it for you to network with others in the workplace? Ten

38. What are some tools you use to maintain relationships with others? Email, text messaging, social media

39. What is your preferred method of communication (email, in person, phone, and so forth)? In person

40. How much energy does it take for you to navigate the corporate or white-collar working environment? A lot of energy

Emotional Intelligence and Introversion/Extroversion Tendency Interview (40 Questions)

Send to Dr. Reginald Ramsey, PhD, MBA, CISA, @ <u>HRTC1906@gmail.com</u>

Name: Female/Black/Professional

Response Date: May 19, 2022

1. What is your official job title? Vice chancellor for institutional accountability and accreditation and professor of law, Southern University Law Center

2. How long have you been in your current role? Three years

3. What attributes or skills helped you to reach your current career level? Strong analytical and logical reasoning skills, strong critical reading and thinking skills, a detailed and goal-oriented work ethic, the ability to work independently and collaboratively

4. What does your typical day entail? Please elaborate as much as possible.

   At the start of my workday, I check email and respond as needed. If it is during the semester, I usually teach a 9 to 10:15 a.m. Constitutional Law course; thus, I spend time before class reviewing for it. After class, I hold office hours until 12:30 p.m. During office hours, if I don't have student appointments, I return phone calls, conduct research, read legal periodicals related to constitutional law and/or current events and updates in higher/law school education, do prep work for the next class, and so forth.

   When I do not have class at 9 a.m., after reviewing and responding to emails, I conference with my assistant for about thirty minutes at the start of each day to discuss tasks that need immediate attention and prioritize tasks for the day, week, and possibly month (if deadlines are approaching). I spend about an hour sending calendar reminders to various department heads about upcoming deadlines and following up with them on the status of various reports associated with said deadlines to ensure that reports are completed and submitted timely. I review, revise, and edit reports from various department heads and return to them for finalization. I spend about two to four hours per day in meetings (with the chancellor, other VCs, department heads, and so forth.). I conduct annual unit planning, evaluations or assessments, and reporting training about two hours per day. I also work on my own reports associated with various objectives and benchmarks; this information is reported to the chancellor, the SUS president, the Louisiana board of regents, our regional accreditor, the Southern Association of Colleges and Schools, the Commission on Colleges (SACSCOC), and the law school accrediting body, the American Bar Association (ABA).

5. How many hours do you work per week? It varies but forty to sixty. However, during accreditation years, hours can average up to about seventy to eighty hours per week.

6. What advice would you give to someone who wants to be in your position someday? Be true to yourself—your values, morals, and beliefs. No position or title is worth sacrificing who you are and what you believe in. While you may experience some setbacks or bumps in the road when you stand up for right, ultimately you will be a better person for not compromising yourself or your values.

7. What has been the role of mentors or coaches in your career advancement? Unfortunately, I don't think I had a true "mentor" in the early years of my career. I also don't think I ever had a "true" or "official" mentor during most of my career. However, in

the last ten years, I have had a few trustworthy senior-level faculty members and administrators who proved to be very supportive and were allies who helped with my career advancement.

8. How many mentors do you have or have had over your career? I've had about six people I have considered to be mentors at various points in my career.

9. How often do you speak or communicate with your mentor or mentors? Not very often these days. During the critical years of my advancement (the five to seven years before my current position), I spoke with them weekly (I almost daily spoke with one mentor, the person who held the position I now currently hold).

10. How do you balance your work with your private life? As much as possible, I give myself at least one day (and I strive for two days) per week when I don't work at all. During stressful accreditation periods, when I have to work every day, I give myself at least two hours per day for prayer, meditation/devotional time, exercise, and so forth. I also make time regularly, at least twice per month, to do something I enjoy with family, friends, and/or my significant other (i.e., a family dinner, a movie, a sporting event, and so forth). Before the pandemic, I traveled a lot, which included at least one international trip per year. I'd like to get back to traveling more.

11. How often do you set goals? I'm not sure I understand the question. I set goals daily, weekly, monthly, yearly, and so forth with respect to work because my job or position is all about deadlines. If you mean on a broader or more personal level, I don't think I set goals outside of items listed in the response to question ten above. I probably should set some post-career goals (i.e., pay off my mortgage within the next ten years, write a book, run a marathon, and so forth).

12. What type of goals do you set (yearly, monthly, and so forth)? Please see my response to question 11.

13. How long have you been working in the market space? I'm not sure what "market space" means. I've had a job since I was sixteen years old. I had my first "legal" job while in law school at age twenty-three. I'm fifty-one now.

14. What was your first job? My first job as a teenager was in a box recycling factory. My first "legal" job was as a "law clerk" at the Louisiana Department of Environmental Quality (where I met and learned so much from my first mentor).

15. What valuable lessons have you learned over your career? I've learned to trust my instincts. More importantly, I have learned to always be able to support everything I write or say with verifiable evidence and empirical data.

16. What type of spiritual life do you have? I start my day with a devotional or inspirational reading and prayer. I pray or talk to God (I have conversations that are different from my "official" prayers) daily. Before the pandemic, I did not attend any church regularly (maybe three or four times per year). During the pandemic, I have come to enjoy "virtual" worship services of various churches.

17. Do you attend or engage in any religious activities? I do not attend in-person services anymore. I do not like the touching (hugging, kissing, embracing, and so forth) that happens at churches. I regularly participate in religious services remotely.

18. What role has emotional intelligence played in your career progression? While I only learned about this term within the last ten years, I believe I have always had high emotional intelligence, which has helped me to maneuver through the various paths of

my career. I think my life experiences while growing up of being bullied, teased, and made to feel like an outsider by many of my peers made me more sensitive to others' feelings and struggles. Even though I've hit a few bumps in the road (facing some aggressive, insensitive, and egotistical opponents), I believe I owe a lot of my success to being able to understand and relate to different people.

19. What are some unwritten rules or norms you learned from being in a white-collar environment? There is a certain amount of "social interaction" unrelated to your specific, assigned job, title, or position that is expected (required) at every job. Always be professional; even at so-called social gatherings or events, remain professional. Even when you disagree with someone, do not be disagreeable. Do not say everything you think. Listen carefully before responding. Often it is best to listen now and respond later (after time for careful deliberation and consultation with a mentor or trusted friend). *Never* hit "reply all." *Never* respond to an email while emotional, angry, hurt, and so forth; instead, draft a response (if you must respond at all) and have a trusted friend or mentor review it before you send it.

20. Did your parents or grandparents work in a white-collar setting? Yes or no? No.

21. Did your parents or grandparents teach you how to navigate a white-collar working environment? No.

22. What did your parents or grandparents teach you about working in a white-collar environment? No.

23. How did you learn about these unwritten rules or norms (observation, mentors, mistakes)? Much of what I have learned in my career has been through experiences (some of which were very unpleasant). Particularly, when I was in a white male-dominated

law firm environment, it was impossible to find a trustworthy and knowledgeable mentor. Later in life, I have had the advantage of having some helpful allies and mentors. Unfortunately, however, as a woman, I have still had to deal with the struggles of trying to succeed in "a male-dominated profession."

24. Currently, how many individuals do you mentor? Four. I probably mentor more than four people (even though only these four probably consider me a mentor), because I regularly provide advice, counsel, and feedback to numerous students and young law professors and attorneys.

25. How often do you listen to or read about successful individuals? Before the pandemic, I tried to read at least one or two biographies or autobiographies per year. Over the last few years, however, I haven't had the time (or motivation) for leisure reading. I have never really been receptive to listening to TED Talks and motivational speakers. None of that motivates me.

26. What role has self-talk played in your career success? Self-talk is and has always been one of the most important components of my success. I am motivated to succeed by my own prior successes. Achieving success reinforces for me that I can achieve anything to which I devote my time, talent, and skills. I start *every* day with positive self-talk and affirmations.

27. How do you motivate yourself each day? See my response to question 26. I really am a self-starter, and I thrive on accomplishing goals set daily, weekly, monthly, and so forth.

28. What are some of your hobbies? I enjoy exercising and riding my bike. I also enjoy volunteering (serving as a judge and grader in debate, mock trials, and moot court competitions). In addition, I enjoy doing DIY projects around my house.

29. Do you believe in the PIE model for career success? Yes, I don't agree with it. However, it is how the corporate game is done. It's more about who you know than what you know.

30. How often do you exercise? I exercise five or six days a week at least forty-five to sixty minutes per session.

31. How much time do you take off each year to recharge your batteries? Before my current position, I took off about three to four weeks per year (at least one or two weeks at the end of each semester). However, in recent years, due to my role serving as the primary liaison with the accreditors for my institution and being involved in three different accreditation reaffirmation processes, I have been able to take only about five to seven days off. However, this year I have plans to take three to four weeks of much-needed annual leave time.

32. May I use your name in the book? Yes.

33. Whom would you recommend I interview for this book? Two of my work colleagues

34. How would you characterize yourself (either introverted or extroverted)? I am an introverted introvert.

35. What introverted or extroverted qualities do you daily display to the general public? I prefer to work alone rather than in groups. I do not enjoy "small talk" or "casual conversations" outside of my very small circle of friend. When I am required to participate in person in meetings, social events, class, and so forth, it is very draining. Thereafter, I recharge through alone time.

36. On a scale of one to ten, with ten being easiest, how easy is it for you to start a conversation with a stranger? I do not start conversations with strangers ever, so it would be a one.

37. On a scale of one to ten, with ten being easiest, how easy is it for you to network with others in the workplace? Over the years, I have learned to network, but it is still very draining and exhausting. I'd rate my ease (or lack thereof) as a four.

38. What are some tools you use to maintain relationships with others? I try to check in regularly either via email or by phone. I promptly return calls, emails, texts, and so forth. I volunteer in areas of interest in my community and the legal profession.

39. What is your preferred method of communication (email, in person, phone, and so forth)? Email is my preferred method of communication.

40. How much energy does it take for you to navigate the corporate or white-collar working environment? Far more energy than I would like. It is quite draining. As a woman and a person of color, it is probably even more uncomfortable than it should be because of the extra energy and effort required to make sure my voice is heard and valued.

Emotional Intelligence and Introversion/Extroversion Tendency Interview (40 Questions)

Send to Dr. Reginald Ramsey, PhD, MBA, CISA, @ HRTC1906@ gmail.com

Name:___Male/Black/Professional_____

Response Date: __5/18/2022_____

1. What is your official job title? Human resources manager

2. How long have you been in your current role? Five years

3. What attributes or skills helped you to reach your current career level? My educational background (I was in finance and accounting) and my understanding of people and how they interact

4. What does your typical day entail? Please elaborate as much as possible. Helping the management team with human resource counseling, dealing with personnel issues, interviewing, managing counseling staff, coaching, taking advantage of opportunities, and conducting disciplinary actions

5. How many hours do you work per week? At least forty, sometimes forty-five or more

6. What advice would you give someone who wants to be in your position someday? Take some courses in physiology and sociology; those will help with human interactions.

7. What has been the role of mentors or coaches in your career advancement? They showed me what an effective HR manager would understand. I learned on the job and didn't get a lot of mentoring. I performed to the best of my abilities.

8. How many mentors do you have or have had over your career? Three to four. I learned and watched them—how they did it.

9. How often do you speak or communicate with your mentor or mentors? Weekly

10. How do you balance your work or life? I moved things around; I did what I had to do to get the job done; I cut down on home or family time. I went home late; I was loyal to the company.

11. How often do you set goals? Yearly

12. What type of goals do you set (yearly, monthly, and so forth)? Yearly professional goals

13. How long have you been working in the market space? Forty-two years plus two years of military

14. What was your first job? Management intern in accounting

15. What valuable lessons have you learned over your career? Be honest, have integrity, and work hard. Work smart; learn from others who have more experience than you.

16. What type of spiritual life do you have? I believe in God; I adhere to values from my home, such as being kind. Treat everyone as humanly as possible. Tell the truth.

17. Do you attend or engage in any religious activities? No

18. What role has emotional intelligence played in your career progression? It helped me to be humble, bear with all the inconsistencies and roadblocks, and be civil. I learned to hold my peace and keep my cool.

19. What are some unwritten rules or norms you learned from being in a white-collar environment? Favoritism exists; legacy exists. Others will try to use you as an example of the liberatism.

20. Did your parents or grandparents work in a white-collar setting? Yes or no? No. Momma and my grandmother were domestic workers; dad/grandfather.

21. Did your parents or grandparents teach you how to navigate a white-collar working environment? No

22. What did your parents or grandparents teach you about working in a white-collar environment? Do it well; be respectful to authority over you.

23. How did you learn about these unwritten rules or norms (observation, mentors, mistakes)? Observations and mistakes

24. Currently, how many individuals do you mentor? None

25. How often do you listen to or read about successful individuals? Often

26. What role has self-talk played in your career success? A very important role; figure out your daily schedule and formulate some ideas to be successful. It helps to finish a task. Help someone on the job.

27. How do you motivate yourself each day? Think about things you need and want for your family. You know the obstacles, so get up. Pay the mortgage or car payments.

28. What are some of your hobbies? Driving Porsches, watching sports (football and basketball, not so much into baseball and softball)

29. Do you believe in the PIE model for career success? Yes

30. How often do you exercise? None

31. How much time do you take off each year to recharge your batteries? Once per year

32. May I use your name in the book? NA

33. Whom would you recommend I interview for this book? NA

34. How would you characterize yourself (either introverted or extroverted)? I was born an introvert, but I'm moving to extrovert.

35. What introverted or extroverted qualities do you daily display to the general public?

    Introverted: I read a lot of books and didn't socialize. I was bashful; I didn't like being in the limelight. I was nervous in the limelight.

    Extrovert: I'm not afraid to walk to a stranger; I've never met a stranger.

36. On a scale of one to ten, with ten being easiest, how easy is it for you to start a conversation with a stranger? Ten

37. On a scale of one to ten, with ten being easiest, how easy is it for you to network with others in the workplace? Ten

38. What are some tools you use to maintain relationships with others? Telephone calls, emails, visits, texts

39. What is your preferred method of communication (email, in person, phone, and so forth)? Telephone

40. How much energy does it take for you to navigate the corporate or white-collar working environment? It is relatively easy but depends on feedback from the other person.

Emotional Intelligence and Introversion/Extroversion Tendency Interview (40 Questions)

Send to Dr. Reginald Ramsey, PhD, MBA, CISA, @ HRTC1906@ gmail.com

Name: Black/Female/Professional

Response Date: 05/04/2022

1. What is your official job title? Medical social service counselor

2. How long have you been in your current role? Seven years

3. What attributes or skills helped you to reach your current career level? Excelling as a writer and communicator, having good grammar, and being proficient in office software and office machines. My typing is superb. I have good recall and am attentive and empathetic. I coordinate scheduling and am organized. I have the ability to serve a diverse multicultural patient population and remain poised under extreme circumstances. I have the ability to facilitate meetings and collaborate effectively with a multidisciplinary medical team and health care providers.

4. What does your typical day entail? Please elaborate as much as possible A typical day as a medical social service counselor involves helping patients and their families navigate the medical system. This role includes doing patient advocacy; completing inpatient psychosocial assessments; setting up nursing home, hospice, and home health psychiatric placement; assessing patients and family members for after-care services and referrals to mental health or intensive outpatient or inpatient substance abuse facilities; and providing short-term counseling and therapy.

5. How many hours do you work per week? Forty-plus hours

6. What advice would you give to someone who wants to be in your position someday? You must enjoy being an advocate and connecting individuals with the appropriate resources. Also be intentional about leaving your work at work.

7. What has been the role of mentors or coaches in your career advancement? Continuing to educate and provide professional development

8. How many mentors do you have or have had over your career? There have been many unbeknownst to me. I have learned from listening and watching people I admire and inspire to become.

9. How often do you speak or communicate with your mentor or mentors? Daily there is inspiration and mentorship.

10. How do you balance your work with your private life? I debrief, compartmentalize, and travel with stillness and gratitude.

11. How often do you set goals? Often, whether it's personal, educational, fitness related, or social

12. What type of goals do you set (yearly, monthly, and so forth)? I set goals year-round ranging from educational goals, fitness goals, or a DIY home project.

13. How long have you been working in the market space? Roughly forty years

14. What was your first job? Cashier at Kmart

15. What valuable lessons have you learned over your career? Build on what you've learned or mastered; be open to alternative approaches. concepts, and others' perspectives.

16. What type of spiritual life do you have? I believe spirituality is an action, merely quoting scripture, and I believe God resides within each of us. My relationship with God is fluid, ever seeking. My treatment of others is a direct reflection of my strong belief: do unto others as you'd wish it be done to you.

17. Do you attend or engage in any religious activities? Yes, but not routinely

18. What role has emotional intelligence played in your career progression? It has given me the ability to control my impulses or emotions during a crisis, recognize my biases, quickly adjust or adapt to various circumstances, intentionally develop meaningful relationships, be direct, demonstrate excellence, listen, and manage conflict.

19. What are some unwritten rules or norms you learned from being in a white-collar environment? Anyone is replaceable. Often office sociability outweighs performance. Try not to outshine your supervisor.

20. Did your parents or grandparents work in a white-collar setting? No, my grandparents had no formal education. And my parents didn't graduate from high school.

21. Did your parents or grandparents teach you how to navigate a white-collar working environment? Whenever possible, demonstrate excellence. Never downplay your intellect.

22. What did your parents or grandparents teach you about working in a white-collar environment? Expect criticism. Never accept an unjust reprimand. Never get too comfortable and reveal private family matters.

23. How did you learn about these unwritten rules or norms (observation, mentors, mistakes)? Experience and observation

24. Currently, how many individuals do you mentor? None

25. How often do you listen to or read about successful individuals? "Successful" is subjective, but at least once a month I read about an interesting person or concept. I just finished reading *Minimalism* by Ryan Nicodemus and *The Joy of Less*.

26. What role has self-talk played in your career success? I practice positive thinking. As a medical social service counselor, I'm often tasked with educating patients and family members about being HIV positive, hospice recommendations, the amputation of limbs, and death. In each situation, the person is fixated on negative thoughts. It's crucial that I let each individual know he or she has the power, opportunity, and chance to overcome and live fully despite the diagnosis.

27. How do you motivate yourself each day? I hate exercising, but I do so every day. Each morning I wake up and have a pep talk with myself; I say to myself, "You're blessed. You get to exercise at home. And do you remember saying to yourself 'If only I had a home gym'? Well, God has blessed you with it. Humans. hey, *get up*. You don't like going to work, *but* you go anyway! So *get up*. You don't have to like exercising, but you're gonna do it anyway!"

28. What are some of your hobbies? I like to read. I like gardening and DIY home projects.

29. Do you believe in the PIE model for career success? Unfortunately, it's not what you know but who you know. "Brown nosing" is often rewarded in the workplace, while talented individuals are actually overlooked.

30. How often do you exercise? Monday through Friday (five days a week) for thirty minutes each time

31. How much time do you take off each year to recharge your batteries? If I'm traveling abroad, I take ten to fourteen days or a four-day trip.

32. May I use your name in the book? Mmmm. Let me think about it.

33. Whom would you recommend I interview for this book? Someone who has achieved what you're trying to achieve

34. How would you characterize yourself (either introverted or extroverted)? I'm both. Professionally, I am an extrovert, and I'm an introvert in my personal space.

35. What introverted or extroverted qualities do you daily display to the general public? Professionally I'm very vocal, hands on, involved, collaborative, and available. On the other hand, my personal space is guarded, quiet, reserved, full of self-care, and intentional.

36. On a scale of one to ten, with ten being easiest, how easy is it for you to start a conversation with a stranger? Ten

37. On a scale of one to ten, with ten being easiest, how easy is it for you to network with others in the workplace? Eight

38. What are tools you use to maintain relationships with others? I email and text to maintain relationships.

39. What is your preferred method of communication (email, in person, phone, and so forth)? I prefer text messages.

40. How much energy does it take for you to navigate the corporate or white-collar working environment? It depends; when you're collaborating with a multidisciplinary team, it can be challenging. Still, I often learn more and enjoy different perspectives.

Emotional Intelligence and Introversion/Extroversion Tendency Interview (40 Questions)

Send to Dr. Reginald Ramsey, PhD, MBA, CISA, @ HRTC1906@ gmail.com

Name:___Black/Female/Professional_____

Response Date: _____6/5/2022_____

1. What is your official job title? Surgical nurse practitioner, adult and geriatrics

2. How long have you been in your current role? Thirteen years

3. What attributes or skills helped you to reach your current career level? A willingness to learn and ask questions when I didn't understand

4. What does your typical day entail? Please elaborate as much as possible. Organizing, planning my day, answering a lot of questions, showing pure servitude, and showing empathy to others

5. How many hours do you work per week? Fifty

6. What advice would you give to someone who wants to be in your position someday? Have a mentor. Sometimes you get burned out. Sometimes we stay too long. Change takes a lot of energy. Do some networking; you need the network to get things accomplished. Don't be an island; it will increase the risk of burnout. Networking helps to change your thought process.

7. What has been the role of mentors or coaches in your career advancement? There is a lack thereof; I don't have a lot of them. I'm an introverted individual; my introversion hurt me. I had to mature; I believe God has helped me. Life circumstances helped to change my mindset; I need to pass it on.

8. How many mentors do you have or have had over your career? One

9. How often do you speak or communicate with your mentor or mentors? Once per year

10. How do you balance your work with your private life? Leave work at work; complete tasks in a timely fashion. Complete all tasks before leaving.

11. How often do you set goals? It depends; financial goals are yearly. Personal goals depend; I set them once per quarter.

12. What type of goals do you set (yearly, monthly, and so forth)? Yearly, quarterly

13. How long have you been working in the market space? Thirty-five years

14. What was your first job? Taco organization, food industry

15. What valuable lessons have you learned over your career? Realize your limitations.

16. What type of spiritual life do you have? Before COVID—got tested. I love the Lord; after COVID, I'm not as diligent as I used to be. I need to recommit.

17. Do you attend or engage in any religious activities? Yes

18. What role has emotional intelligence played in your career progression? Life changes have taught me patience. I have a brother with mental health issues. I lost my mom and grandmom; I have become the family matriarch.

19. What are some unwritten rules or norms you learned from being in a white-collar environment? There is a different set of rules for black and white people. You are always subject to your white peers. Black views are not as valued as those of white peers.

20. Did your parents or grandparents work in a white-collar setting? Yes or no? No

21. Did your parents or grandparents teach you how to navigate a white-collar working environment? No

22. What did your parents or grandparents teach you about working in a white-collar environment? Promptness, commitment, dedication. These gave me a work ethic and morals.

23. How did you learn about these unwritten rules or norms (observation, mentors, mistakes)? All of the above

24. Currently, how many individuals do you mentor? Two

25. How often do you listen to or read about successful individuals? Frequently, monthly

26. What role has self-talk played in your career success? Various. God helped me. I use Post-it notes and reminders. I set objectives.

27. How do you motivate yourself each day? It's a process, a fight within myself.

28. What are some of your hobbies? Swimming, working out at the gym, doing things with nieces and nephews, helping young people develop

29. Do you believe in the PIE model for career success? Perceptions make a difference.

30. How often do you exercise? Four days per week

31. How much time do you take off each year to recharge your batteries? Four weeks

32. May I use your name in the book? Keep confidential.

33. Whom would you recommend I interview for this book?

34. How would you characterize yourself (either introverted or extroverted)? I have a mixture of both. I'm personally introverted; I can't take a lot of noise.

35. What introverted or extroverted qualities do you daily display to the general public?

    Introverted—I read the room. I don't speak until I know the atmosphere. I'm comfortable alone.

36. On a scale of one to ten, with ten being easiest, how easy is it for you to start a conversation with a stranger? It depends on the atmosphere. I'm about a five; I used to be a zero before my mom passed.

37. On a scale of one to ten, with ten being easiest, how easy is it for you to network with others in the workplace? Three or four

38. What are some tools you use to maintain relationships with others? Offering encouragement; staying positive; keeping a positive outlook; and doing texts, chats, and check-ins

39. What is your preferred method of communication (email, in person, phone, and so forth)? Phone

40. How much energy does it take for you to navigate the corporate or white-collar working environment? Too much; it takes a lot of energy.

Emotional Intelligence and Introversion/Extroversion Tendency Interview (40 Questions)

Send to Dr. Reginald Ramsey, PhD, MBA, CISA, @ HRTC1906@ gmail.com

Name:__Black/Female/Professional_____

Response Date: ___7/1/2022_____

1. What is your official job title? Senior product manager

2. How long have you been in your current role? Eleven months

3. What attributes or skills helped you to reach your current career level? Good organizational skills, business acuteness, knowledge of cloud-based solutions, and project management

4. What does your typical day entail? Please elaborate as much as possible. Checking and responding to emails, viewing project check-ins, reviewing and finalizing presentations, sitting in on team calls, attending one-on-one meetings with a manager, and addressing open problems with the development team

5. How many hours do you work per week? Fifty to sixty

6. What advice would you give to someone who wants to be in your position someday? Ask the person what his or her favorite subjects are. If he or she has a professional personality and business and technical acuteness, then choose an undergraduate major in engineering, biomedical, or mechanical engineering degrees; however, for the graduate level, I would recommend a master's degree in business or management of technology.

7. What has been the role of mentors or coaches in your career advancement? They helped me to position my career, to define

my career path, and to understand my career and identify roles for my progression in my career. They helped to process issues.

8. How many mentors do you have or have had over your career? About seven

9. How often do you speak or communicate with your mentor or mentors? I meet with one mentor every six weeks.

10. How do you balance your work with your private life? I'm single with no kids. I take a run or exercise in the evenings. I socialize with friends on the weekends.

11. How often do you set goals? I set goals two to three times per week. I set big goals twice per year.

12. What type of goals do you set (yearly, monthly, and so forth)? Weekly, quarterly, and yearly

13. How long have you been working in the market space? Twenty-two years

14. What was your first job? Lawn care telemarketing

15. What valuable lessons have you learned over your career? Relationships are key. They help to navigate your career. Communication tone and style are important; you need to sound right. How you present yourself is important. Look the part and know your stuff. You need emotional intelligence. Adjust to the situation. Stay well read. Know your craft.

16. What type of spiritual life do you have? Daily communication or prayer with God. God has come through. I listen to the Bible and different pastors; COVID-19 changed me.

17. Do you attend or engage in any religious activities? Not right now because of COVID-19; in general I would.

18. What role has emotional intelligence played in your career progression? I'm not the best at emotional intelligence. I had a good relationship with my manager at the time; I learned not to show an attitude when I disagreed; I learned to pause and ask more clarification questions.

19. What are some unwritten rules or norms you learned from being in a white-collar environment? I can't show my ethical side. I can't wear my hair as I want. The company is more diversity aware. I don't have as much freedom with budgeting, flights, food, and so forth. I take calls on the road; I've got to deliver.

20. Did your parents or grandparents work in a white-collar setting? Yes or no? My mom was a banker over customer service. My dad was a respiratory therapist.

21. Did your parents or grandparents teach you how to navigate a white-collar working environment? No

22. What did your parents or grandparents teach you about working in a white-collar environment? Do your work; do your job.

23. How did you learn about these unwritten rules or norms (observation, mentors, mistakes)? Observations. I follow what others do.

24. Currently, how many individuals do you mentor? Five

25. How often do you listen to or read about successful individuals? If I do things on Facebook or LinkedIn, I will look; I could improve in this area.

26. What role has self-talk played in your career success? I believe that if you tell yourself you can do it, you can do it. It helps to hype yourself up. It helps to manage your nervousness. Speak clearly. Pray beforehand; this plays a big role.

27. How do you motivate yourself each day? Through self-talk; I'm a goal-oriented person. I'm aware of my potential to lose my temper; I'm still working on it.

28. What are some of your hobbies? Running, going out to eat, attending concerts and plays, volunteering

29. Do you believe in the PIE model for career success? Yes

30. How often do you exercise? Three to four times per week on average

31. How much time do you take off each year to recharge your batteries? Twenty-one days plus vacations (three weeks)

32. May I use your name in the book? Keep confidential.

33. Whom would you recommend I interview for this book?

34. How would you characterize yourself (either introverted or extroverted)? Introverted

35. What introverted or extroverted qualities do you daily display to the general public?

    Introverted—I like to work alone. I make myself talk to others in a social gathering. I stay in the corner alone. Extroverted—I can work in a team; I can work with others.

36. On a scale of one to ten, with ten being easiest, how easy is it for you to start a conversation with a stranger? Six. I use self-talk.

37. On a scale of one to ten, with ten being easiest, how easy is it for you to network with others in the workplace? Six. It's not easy for me, but it is needed.

38. What are some tools you use to maintain relationships with others? Telephone. I call others I know. I text.

39. What is your preferred method of communication (email, in person, phone, and so forth)? Phone

40. How much energy does it take for you to navigate the corporate or white-collar working environment? It takes medium-level energy to navigate the company.

CHAPTER 6

SURVEY RESPONSES: MANAGEMENT PROFESSIONALS

Emotional Intelligence and Introversion/Extroversion Tendency Interview (40 Questions)

Send to Dr. Reginald Ramsey, PhD, MBA, CISA, @ HRTC1906@ gmail.com

Name:___Black/Male/Manager_____

Response Date: __5/16/2022_____

1. What is your official job title? Marketing director, global sales consultancy

2. How long have you been in your current role? Two months

3. What attributes or skills helped you to reach your current career level? I'm comfortable with being uncomfortable. Skills include marketing and creativity. Be open to failure; most of us are failing fast. Be a curious individual. Be courageous. I'm a product of my parents.

4. What does your typical day entail? Please elaborate as much as possible. I lead a team of marketers; I'm a digital experience manager over a small team. I'm a strategy person. I manage the financials, marketing, and internal business. I help my team as a marketing tech. I check on my team members. I do reporting and presentations. I work with partners and vendors in tasks involving product releases and corporate strategy development. I work with executive representatives for marketing. There are lots of meetings; I'm part of the management team.

5. How many hours do you work per week? Forty-five

6. What advice would you give to someone who wants to be in your position someday? Learn to delegate with intention. Teach new skills. Relationship building is huge. Understand what motivates and excites others. Diverse thinking is critical.

7. What has been the role of mentors or coaches in your career advancement? Huge. I like my therapists. I'm half introverted and half extroverted.

8. How many mentors do you have or have had over your career? Approximately three

9. How often do you speak or communicate with your mentor or mentors? Every two weeks, monthly

10. How do you balance your work with your private life? I do gym in the morning, my day job, and gym again. Then I spend time with my partner.

11. How often do you set goals? Every quarter

12. What type of goals do you set (yearly, monthly, and so forth)? Professional goals are quarterly. Personal goals are three times per year.

13. How long have you been working in the market space? Ten to twelve years

14. What was your first job? Working at a tuxedo shop

15. What valuable lessons have you learned over your career? Many. Don't be afraid to fail. Be open to learning; this means falling on your face sometimes.

16. What type of spiritual life do you have? I'm a Christian.

17. Do you attend or engage in any religious activities? I do online services.

18. What role has emotional intelligence played in your career progression? It is very helpful. It helped me to get out of my own skin and overcome my shyness. I have grown so much as an individual.

19. What are some unwritten rules or norms you learned from being in a white-collar environment? Manage microaggressions.

20. Did your parents or grandparents work in a white-collar setting? Yes or no? Grandparents—no, parents—yes.

21. Did your parents or grandparents teach you how to navigate a white-collar working environment? To take the first step, don't be afraid to take risks … Try it …

22. What did your parents or grandparents teach you about working in a white-collar environment?

23. How did you learn about these unwritten rules or norms (observation, mentors, mistakes)? All of the above

24. Currently, how many individuals do you mentor? None

25. How often do you listen to or read about successful individuals? All the time. I listen to the *How I Built This* podcast.

26. What role has self-talk played in your career success? It has a huge role; I have a pep talk every day.

27. How do you motivate yourself each day? I designed my office to show my why. I have a library of books, including marketing books. I drink coffee. I develop my clear plan daily.

28. What are some of your hobbies? I love traveling and going to new countries. I'm a foodie who enjoys shopping, men's fashions, architecture, music, the clarinet, and the symphony. I enjoy going out to eat. I enjoy the bar and craft drinks.

29. Do you believe in the PIE model for career success? Performance and exposure, yes. I also believe in image (new age of fashion for executives ... new looks).

30. How often do you exercise? Five days per week

31. How much time do you take off each year to recharge your batteries? Four weeks

32. May I use your name in the book? NA

33. Whom would you recommend I interview for this book? NA

34. How would you characterize yourself (either introverted or extroverted)? Half and half. I can turn on ... I need to recharge alone while listening to music.

35. What introverted or extroverted qualities do you daily display to the general public?

    Extroverted—I can have a conversation with anyone; I love to get to know people.

Introverted—I like to be home and have quiet time. I enjoy being alone with music and me time. I like getting haircuts and spa treatments.

36. On a scale of one to ten, with ten being easiest, how easy is it for you to start a conversation with a stranger? Ten

37. On a scale of one to ten, with ten being easiest, how easy is it for you to network with others in the workplace? Ten

38. What are some tools you use to maintain relationships with others? Instagram, LinkedIn, Facebook, TikTok, and FaceTime; Twitter not so much.

39. What is your preferred method of communication (email, in person, phone, and so forth)? In person

40. How much energy does it take for you to navigate the corporate or white-collar working environment? A lot of energy; it is exhausting.

Emotional Intelligence and Introversion/Extroversion Tendency Interview (40 Questions)

Send to Dr. Reginald Ramsey, PhD, MBA, CISA, @ HRTC1906@gmail.com

Name:_Black/Female/Manager ___

Response Date: ___May 3, 2022_____

1. What is your official job title? Legal business consultant/growth coach

2. How long have you been in your current role? 2015; 2019, full-time

3. What attributes or skills helped you to reach your current career level? I have a legal background; I managed law firms. I have paralegal skills.

4. What does your typical day entail? Please elaborate as much as possible. It varies, with emails, client contracts, consulting sessions, social media, and networking.

5. How many hours do you work per week? Approximately seventy

6. What advice would you give to someone who wants to be in your position someday? Ask for help. Build a team.

7. What has been the role of mentors or coaches in your career advancement? In a law firm, I had no coaches or mentors. I became the trainer. I met my business partner. He became my accountability partner. I still maintain two coaches or mentors.

8. How many mentors do you have or have had over your career? Two

9. How often do you speak or communicate with your mentor or mentors? Every week

10. How do you balance your work with your private life? I'm always working. When I'm out with my girls, I'm still working. I partnered with someone from Atlanta.

11. How often do you set goals? Quarterly, monthly, and weekly. Also, I do mastermind sessions every quarter.

12. What type of goals do you set (yearly, monthly, and so forth)? Quarterly, monthly, and weekly

13. How long have you been working in the market space? Seven years

14. What was your first job? Internship right out of high school; I went every summer. It was an aluminum company. I created a newsletter, wrote SOPs, and did cost analysis.

15. What valuable lessons have you learned over your career? Your network is your net worth; not all money is good money.

16. What type of spiritual life do you have? I very much have one; I'm in church every Sunday.

17. Do you attend or engage in any religious activities? Yes

18. What role has emotional intelligence played in your career progression? It's the cornerstone of my business. I'm cognitive of this with my clients. I believe in missions, visions, and values. I pay attention to energy.

19. What are some unwritten rules or norms you learned from being in a white-collar environment? You have to read the room. Know who you are talking to; wear a mask.

20. Did your parents or grandparents work in a white-collar setting? Yes or no? No

21. Did your parents or grandparents teach you how to navigate a white-collar working environment? No

22. What did your parents or grandparents teach you about working in a white-collar environment? Work hard. Play the game.

23. How did you learn about these unwritten rules or norms (observation, mentors, mistakes)? Observations

24. Currently, how many individuals do you mentor? I'm coaching two; also there is a group of four ladies.

25. How often do you listen to or read about successful individuals? Every day

26. What role has self-talk played in your career success? It is crucial to my success. Mental health is important to me.

27. How do you motivate yourself each day? Knowing I'm in control. I love to travel.

28. What are some of your hobbies? Traveling, reading, writing, painting, and spending time with kids and friends

29. Do you believe in the PIE model for career success? I most certainly do! I 1000 percent believe it!

30. How often do you exercise? Two to three times per week

31. How much time do you take off each year to recharge your batteries? Once every ninety days

32. May I use your name in the book? NA

33. Whom would you recommend I interview for this book? NA

34. How would you characterize yourself (either introverted or extroverted)? Balanced. I love people. Extroverted—I will reserve myself and push myself.

35. What introverted or extroverted qualities do you daily display to the general public? Introverted—I can be quiet. Extroverted—I can talk to anyone in the room and keep a conversation going. I have worked the room.

36. On a scale of one to ten, with ten being easiest, how easy is it for you to start a conversation with a stranger? Eight. I had to get over the hesitation.

37. On a scale of one to ten, with ten being easiest, how easy is it for you to network with others in the workplace? Ten

38. What are some tools you use to maintain relationships with others? Checking in

39. What is your preferred method of communication (email, in person, phone, and so forth)? Phone or text message

40. How much energy does it take for you to navigate the corporate or white-collar working environment? This side is easy; it was tough without a job title.

Emotional Intelligence and Introversion/Extroversion Tendency Interview (40 Questions)

Send to Dr. Reginald Ramsey, PhD, MBA, CISA, @ <u>HRTC1906@gmail.com</u>

Name:_____Black/Female/Manager_____

Response Date: _____13MAY2022_____

1. What is your official job title? President

2. How long have you been in your current role? Three years

3. What attributes or skills helped you to reach your current career level? Over twenty-five years of clinical development and quality systems design and implementation

4. What does your typical day entail? Please elaborate as much as possible.

a. Assess the status of deliverables for contracted clients.
b. Follow up with clients as needed.
c. Complete contracted work.
d. Research regulations, guidance, and industry practices by reviewing slides and attending conferences and webinars.
e. Answer follow-up client questions.

6. How many hours do you work per week? Twenty to thirty

7. What advice would you give to someone who wants to be in your position someday?

   Begin the work now by broadening your network and establishing your credibility in the targeted area.

8. What has been the role of mentors or coaches in your career advancement?

   My mentors supported me by ensuring I was exposed to and contributed to work that would allow me to engage with potential future clients. For example, although my area of expertise is GCP, I was invited to colead a workshop with my GMP counterpart at a GMP conference. This had never been done before, but my contributions and the level of engagement of the audience and conference producers were highly valued. I taught the GMP experts about GCPs.

9. How many mentors do you have or have had over your career? While I was at a large pharma company, I had five pretty consistently. I now feel comfortable saying I have one.

10. How often do you speak or communicate with your mentor or mentors? While at a large pharma company, I proactively scheduled quarterly meetings with each individual at the beginning of the year.

11. How do you balance your work with your private life? I work only twenty or so hours a week.

12. How often do you set goals? NA

13. What type of goals do you set (yearly, monthly, and so forth)? NA

14. How long have you been working in the market space? Over twenty-five years

15. What was your first job? Clinical research assistant for cochlear implant research at Riley Hospital

16. What valuable lessons have you learned over your career? In my early days, I came to work and did my job. I didn't really talk about myself or my personal life. Then two years into my first professional job, it was brought to my attention that no one knew anything about me other than work-related matters. They didn't know I had an eight-year-old son. From that point forward, I scheduled a lunch with everyone on the clinical team so I could share some things about myself. I told them all the exact same thing, but in their minds, I was now approachable because they knew something about me.

17. What type of spiritual life do you have? NA

18. Do you attend or engage in any religious activities? No

19. What role has emotional intelligence played in your career progression? Earlier in my career, I didn't realize the importance of EI or even understand it. Over the years, I came to realize people valued my self-awareness.

20. What are some unwritten rules or norms you learned from being in a white-collar environment? It's not only what you know but who you know. While mentors have the ability to influence your

career, they sometimes won't, whereas a sponsor has the ability and is willing to influence your career.

21. Did your parents or grandparents work in a white-collar setting? Yes or no? No

22. Did your parents or grandparents teach you how to navigate a white-collar working environment? No

23. What did your parents or grandparents teach you about working in a white-collar environment? Nothing

24. How did you learn about these unwritten rules or norms (observation, mentors, mistakes)? Mentors and observations

25. Currently, how many individuals do you mentor? More than five

26. How often do you listen to or read about successful individuals? Never

27. What role has self-talk played in your career success? None

28. How do you motivate yourself each day? I focus on my long-range goal—that is not my career focus.

29. What are some of your hobbies? Reading, traveling, and meeting new people

30. Do you believe in the PIE model for career success? I'm not sure I believe in it for your career success. I think PIE speaks more to your morals and value system.

31. How often do you exercise? Five days a week

32. How much time do you take off each year to recharge your batteries? More than eight days per year

33. May I use your name in the book? NA

34. Whom would you recommend I interview for this book? NA

35. How would you characterize yourself (either introverted or extroverted)? I think I'm a chameleon (a lizard that changes colors to blend in with the environment). I can be what I need to be. I like to think I'm an introvert, but no one believes me.

36. What introverted or extroverted qualities do you daily display to the general public? When I enter the room, I unknowingly make an entrance—smiling, meeting people's eyes, and speaking to everyone. I do this because that is what people expect. This being said, I am quite content, though, not to enter the room and to stay to myself.

37. On a scale of one to ten, with ten being easiest, how easy is it for you to start a conversation with a stranger? Ten. I can talk to anyone about anything for as long as he or she wants to talk about it.

38. On a scale of one to ten, with ten being easiest, how easy is it for you to network with others in the workplace? Ten. I think I am very skilled with this. One of my former mentors described my networking as "a pragmatic approach" to networking.

39. What are some tools you use to maintain relationships with others?

I use different types of relationship tools, ranging from network, job coach, mentor champion, and leader of potential job area interest. At the end of each year, I scheduled lunch, breakfast, or a coffee break with each person at frequencies defined by my relationship with him or her. For example, I met with mentors and sponsors quarterly. I met the leader of a potential job area of interest two times per year to make sure I was on top of his or her mind as he or she was considering resource options.

40. What is your preferred method of communication (email, in person, phone, and so forth)? Any is fine.

41. How much energy does it take for you to navigate the corporate or white-collar working environment? It was exhausting because the culture wasn't my natural state. I always felt like I was "on." Again, I think I was very pragmatic about it, in that I was friendly to everyone because I realized I needed every person I worked with to be successful at my job. Although I was friendly to everyone, I could count on one hand the people I considered my friends.

Emotional Intelligence and Introversion/Extroversion Tendency Interview (40 Questions)

Send to Dr. Reginald Ramsey, PhD, MBA, CISA, @ HRTC1906@gmail.com

Name:___Female/Black/Manager_____

Response Date: __5/18/2022_____

1. What is your official job title? Principal and K-2 teacher

2. How long have you been in your current role? Six years as principal, fifteen years as a teacher

3. What attributes or skills helped you to reach your current career level? I love children; this is what makes me. I love teaching.

4. What does your typical day entail? Please elaborate as much as possible. I get up at 6 a.m. and go to school by 7 a.m. I walk through and pray in every classroom. At 7:30 a.m. I pray with

the staff. At 7:45 a.m. I welcome the students. At 8:15 a.m. class starts with Bible, math, and other typical subjects. I teach students from 8:15 a.m. to 3 p.m. At 3 p.m., I start the principal job. I secure the building, close out the day, and grade papers.

5. How many hours do you work per week? Sixty-plus hours

6. What advice would you give to someone who wants to be in your position someday? It's not easy. There are hard decisions. Life is stressful with moody people. Go for it!

7. What has been the role of mentors or coaches in your career advancement? I had a lot of people who coached me. I wanted to give up, but my coaches encouraged me and prayed for me.

8. How many mentors do you have or have had over your career? Six

9. How often do you speak or communicate with your mentor or mentors? Daily

10. How do you balance your work with your private life? I had to learn to do it; it was all work. Now I make things happen. I go to sleep by 9 p.m. and get proper sleep. No chips; I eat healthily. I walk every morning and resist being around toxic friends and family.

11. How often do you set goals? Just recently I started setting goals. I plan to finish my master's degree in 1.5 years. My next goal is to open my own school.

12. What type of goals do you set (yearly, monthly, and so forth)? Daily goals and short-term goals (in three to five years or ten years)

13. How long have you been working in the market space? Since I was sixteen years old

14. What was your first job? I had a summer job, a work-study program; it was my first time working.

15. What valuable lessons have you learned over your career? Keep pushing, keep moving, stay positive, and be around positive people.

16. What type of spiritual life do you have? I'm very spiritual; I like going to church. I believe in personal devotion.

17. Do you attend or engage in any religious activities? Yes

18. What role has emotional intelligence played in your career progression? EI was not a big role. I was weak; I cried about everything. Now I'm more mature; it made me stronger.

19. What are some unwritten rules or norms you learned from being in a white-collar environment? You can't trust everybody. Read a person. Be very observant; watch your environment.

20. Did your parents or grandparents work in a white-collar setting? Yes or no? No

21. Did your parents or grandparents teach you how to navigate a white-collar working environment? Nothing

22. What did your parents or grandparents teach you about working in a white-collar environment? Nothing

23. How did you learn about these unwritten rules or norms (observation, mentors, mistakes)? All of the above

24. Currently, how many individuals do you mentor? Four

25. How often do you listen to or read about successful individuals? More now because of my mentor's influence and encouragement

26. What role has self-talk played in your career success? It helps to motivate me; it works better early in the morning.

27. How do you motivate yourself each day? I focus on goals.

28. What are some of your hobbies? Walking, exercising, watching old movies, and playing games on my phone

29. Do you believe in the PIE model for career success? Yes

30. How often do you exercise? Daily

31. How much time do you take off each year to recharge your batteries? That's my problem.

32. May I use your name in the book? NA

33. Whom would you recommend I interview for this book? NA

34. How would you characterize yourself (either introverted or extroverted)? Introverted

35. What introverted or extroverted qualities do you daily display to the general public?

    I'm shy at times. I will not hold a conversation. I can get along with anyone.

36. On a scale of one to ten, with ten being easiest, how easy is it for you to start a conversation with a stranger? One … It's not easy.

37. On a scale of one to ten, with ten being easiest, how easy is it for you to network with others in the workplace? Ten

38. What are some tools you use to maintain relationships with others? Be open and honest. Build trust.

39. What is your preferred method of communication (email, in person, phone, and so forth)? Phone

40. How much energy does it take for you to navigate the corporate or white-collar working environment? It takes all my energy.

Emotional Intelligence and Introversion/Extroversion Tendency Interview (40 Questions)

Send to Dr. Reginald Ramsey, PhD, MBA, CISA, @ HRTC1906@ gmail.com

Name:___White/Male/Manager_____

Response Date: _____June 17, 2022_____

1. What is your official job title? Director of user experience design

2. How long have you been in your current role? I have had my current title for one year, but I have led the user experience team for nine years.

3. What attributes or skills helped you to reach your current career level? UX research and UX design skills, collaboration, flexibility, integrity, and track record of success

4. What does your typical day entail? Please elaborate as much as possible. Most days include team stand-up. My job demands management or proposal development, oversite or feedback on team engagements or projects, mentoring (weekly) one-on-one with my manager, engagement with peers and others via e-mail or MS teams, and planning or strategic work.

5. How many hours do you work per week? About fifty

6. What advice would you give to someone who wants to be in your position someday? Learn a wide breadth of UX design and user research techniques, including academic foundations. Couple those with business strategy, leadership, and teamwork. Roll up your sleeves and do the real work.

7. What has been the role of mentors or coaches in your career advancement? It is pretty minimal quite honestly. Most of my career advancement and development has come through my accomplishments or work, the associated learning or reflection, and several really good managers and peers. I'd say some friends have been great mentors, but I have never been part of any formal mentoring program (as a mentee). It's never been offered to me, and I've never sought it out.

8. How many mentors do you have or have had over your career? Formal or official mentors would be zero. Informal (friends, peers, managers) mentors would probably be around twelve. I had a life coach I hired and worked with for about a year, but that was focused more on personal or life growth, not professional growth.

9. How often do you speak or communicate with your mentor or mentors? Infrequently

10. How do you balance your work with your personal life? I work to set boundaries between my professional life and personal life. I really enjoy my work, but my whole life is rich beyond what I do to earn a paycheck. Planning and taking vacations are important, as is making time for family, friends, and myself. I had multiple jobs earlier in my career; that sucked the life and time out of me, so I've learned to work myself into a career or position where excessive overtime, stress, and unrealistic expectations can be minimized.

11. How often do you set goals? In my personal life, I set goals annually and review them regularly throughout the year. At work

I set goals annually and revisit or adjust them quarterly (since the work my team and I do is very dynamic and always shifting).

12. What type of goals do you set (yearly, monthly, and so forth)? In my personal life, I set annual goals (some are within-the-next-five-years goals). As mentioned above, for the most part, my goals at work are annual with quarterly updates. I usually have a three-year team strategy, which is more of a goal framework that provides structure, shape, or intent over time for the entire team.

13. How long have you been working in the market space? I've worked in a "real" job for over thirty-two years.

14. What was your first job? I worked during high school during undergrad (to have spending money) and worked during graduate school to pay my own way. But my first professional job was working for Electronic Data Systems in a systems developer engineering program.

15. What valuable lessons have you learned over your career? So many! A few come to mind: When people show you who they really are, believe them. Hiring the right people for your team is one of the most important things you do. It's important (and rewarding) to help others grow as professionals and as people. The best way to influence is to do the work, not just talk about the work. The skills I use every day are active listening, storytelling, doing written communication, and being humorous.

16. What type of spiritual life do you have? I'm not a religious person. However, I draw spiritual inspiration and connection from visual arts, music, design, and nature.

17. Do you attend or engage in any religious activities? No

18. What role has emotional intelligence played in your career progression? I'd say I have above-average emotional intelligence, and I've deepened it over my career. It has been an essential component of success for me (especially since I didn't have any formal mentors, which means I had to rely on my own savvy, judgment, and advice. I made a lot of mistakes, but I get better all the time.

19. What are some unwritten rules or norms you learned from being in a white-collar environment? It's important to know who the decision maker is. There are many ways to influence. Stick to the facts. No one is irreplaceable. How you treat people is what will be remembered most. Be humble. Take a chance on people, good ideas, and yourself.

20. Did your parents or grandparents work in a white-collar setting? Yes or no? No, none of them did.

21. Did your parents or grandparents teach you how to navigate a white-collar working environment? No

22. What did your parents or grandparents teach you about working in a white-collar environment? Nothing. The white-collar work world was a mystery to my parents. But they always encouraged me to get an education and strive for success in life.

23. How did you learn about these unwritten rules or norms (observation, mentors, mistakes)? Watching people, listening, doing trial and error, and reflecting when things went well or poorly at work to get a sense of "why" and what to do or not to do going forward. I was the youngest kid in my family, so I grew up learning from the successes and mistakes of my siblings.

24. Currently, how many individuals do you mentor? Despite never having a formal mentor, I'm a big believer in mentoring. I'm

currently mentoring six people formally and probably ten to fifteen informally or infrequently.

25. How often do you listen to or read about successful individuals? Occasionally. I was more interested earlier in my career.

26. What role has self-talk played in your career success? It's probably had a small role, mostly since I worked through particularly difficult moments or work challenges.

27. How do you motivate yourself each day? I've always been a very motivated person. It's easy at the moment because I really enjoy my work and team, and I'm in a very good spot in life.

28. What are some of your hobbies? Traveling, wine tasting (including sommelier training), enjoying jazz, being in nature (oceans, mountains, trees), going to art museums, attending live performances (including annual trips to see Broadway performances), spending time with family and friends, and finding novel, quirky, or off-beat experiences

29. Do you believe in the PIE model for career success? Not at all

30. How often do you exercise? Three times per week

31. How much time do you take off each year to recharge your batteries? About six to eight weeks now, depending on the year

32. May I use your name in the book? Yes

33. Whom would you recommend I interview for this book? I think you should interview creative professionals, such as artists, writers, animators, designers, and so forth.

34. How would you characterize yourself (either introverted or extroverted)? I've always had characteristics of both introverts and

extroverts. When I was younger, I was slightly more extroverted. Now I would say I'm slightly more introverted.

35. What introverted or extroverted qualities do you daily display to the general public? I can be very friendly and adventurous but also quiet and alone.

36. On a scale of one to ten, with ten being easiest, how easy is it for you to start a conversation with a stranger? Four

37. On a scale of one to ten, with ten being easiest, how easy is it for you to network with others in the workplace? Six (though "networking" in the workplace isn't something I put much energy into these days)

38. What are some tools you use to maintain relationships with others? I check in regularly with a set of friends, peers, or colleagues I enjoy knowing and/or want to stay connected with. Most of the time I'm the one who initiates the contact, but it's always fun for both.

39. What is your preferred method of communication (email, in person, phone, and so forth)? E-mail, texting, and in person

40. How much energy does it take for you to navigate the corporate or white-collar working environment? It took a lot of energy when I worked in Indiana (a lot). Working in California requires far less. It's so much easier to be authentic and open where I work now. It still requires energy in some situations or projects, but on the whole, I put my energy into my work and my team, not into "navigating the environment."

CHAPTER 7

SURVEY RESPONSES: WHITE-COLLAR EXECUTIVES

Emotional Intelligence and Introversion/Extroversion Tendency Interview (40 Questions)

Send to Dr. Reginald Ramsey, PhD, MBA, CISA, @ <u>HRTC1906@ gmail.com</u>

Name:___ White/Male/Executive_____

Response Date: ___7/20/2022_____

1. What is your official job title? Senior director

2. How long have you been in your current role? Four years

3. What attributes or skills helped you to reach your current career level? The ability to deliver. I connect with people to get things done, know the business, engage with people, and hold relevant conversations with others.

4. What does your typical day entail? Please elaborate as much as possible. Going to meetings, helping to make sure processes are

working, working with other teams, working with my team, reviewing contracts, reading contracts, making adjustments on contracts, and supervising people

5. How many hours do you work per week? Fifty to fifty-five hours. I'm the coach of a cycling team. I have to manage strong personalities. "Shut up, gang. I am going to tell you what we are going to do."

6. What advice would you give to someone who wants to be in your position someday? Learn the business, learn your trade, develop your skills, get an assignment in the business (six-month assignment), ask lots of questions, summon the courage to ask questions from the business, and listen to what others do daily.

7. What has been the role of mentors or coaches in your career advancement? Early on, their role was highly impactful right out of college. They taught me how to be in the workforce and how to interact. They drew me out of my shell and coached me on mistakes, helping me to redirect. I don't have many formal mentors now; I could use help with coaching.

8. How many mentors do you have or have had over your career? Twelve or so

9. How often do you speak or communicate with your mentor or mentors? It varies; it was topical. I was talking daily. Now it's not so much.

10. How do you balance your work with your private life? Before COVID, I led bike rides. I stepped out of work, did something different, cut the grass, or took a walk. I have concrete stopping points. I do things with family.

11. How often do you set goals? At a minimum annually

12. What type of goals do you set (yearly, monthly, and so forth)? I have a daily to-do list.

13. How long have you been working in the market space? Since I was eleven or forty-three years. I carried newspapers and had two paper routes. I cut grass and worked at a fast-food restaurant.

14. What was your first job? My first W-2 job was at a fast-food restaurant.

15. What valuable lessons have you learned over your career? Take opportunities when they are presented. Don't shy away. Do the work. Work hard and get rewarded. Work hard and get noticed. You've got to do the work. I had to say goodbye to some folks early in my career. Some folks said they wouldn't come in. It is an everyday job; politics are part of the job.

16. What type of spiritual life do you have? I'm a practicing Catholic; my son is enrolled to be a Catholic priest.

17. Do you attend or engage in any religious activities? Yes

18. What role has emotional intelligence played in your career progression? It's there; I work on my emotional intelligence. I had low EI during my youth or early career. Over time I have gotten more mature; I learn how to "read" people. I stop acting like I know everything.

19. What are some unwritten rules or norms you learned from being in a white-collar environment? There are a lot of them, including how to dress and how you carry yourself. There are lots of alignments with the values of the business. Align personal values with those of the company. Be vulnerable sometimes; don't blame others.

20. Did your parents or grandparents work in a white-collar setting? Yes or no? Yes, my parents did. My grandparents didn't. My

parents had no college. They worked technical jobs. My mom was a bookkeeper. My dad was a design technician; he drew up plans for engineers and did drafting.

21. Did your parents or grandparents teach you how to navigate a white-collar working environment? No

22. What did your parents or grandparents teach you about working in a white-collar environment? Respect your elders and people. Behave to be invited back. Be polite. Be kind. Be helpful. Ask how you can help. Don't be lazy. Good family values are important.

23. How did you learn about these unwritten rules or norms (observation, mentors, mistakes)? All of the above. Obey the rules if possible; I had to adjust from college. I learned how to behave in meetings. It was "too quiet" in meetings. Learn to step up and speak out. Prepare ahead of time.

24. Currently, how many individuals do you mentor? Twenty-four or so

25. How often do you listen to or read about successful individuals? Not that often

26. What role has self-talk played in your career success? I don't do a lot; I do a lot of visualization. For example, how will a bike ride go? How do I prepare for a meeting? I visualize my day. I don't do self-criticism.

27. How do you motivate yourself each day? I take the first step. The secret is to do the first thing. Don't worry; just start the project or activities. Get over the hump and start the project; get over the inertia.

28. What are some of your hobbies? Cycling, photography, racquetball, yard work, painting, and home projects

29. Do you believe in the PIE model for career success? Yes

30. How often do you exercise? Often, daily

31. How much time do you take off each year to recharge your batteries? Three weeks

32. May I use your name in the book? NA

33. Whom would you recommend I interview for this book? NA

34. How would you characterize yourself (either introverted or extroverted)? Introverted

35. What introverted or extroverted qualities do you daily display to the general public?

    Introverted qualities—I spend time alone in my office, am focused on work, and am not a social butterfly. I enjoy doing puzzles. I used to be shy in high school. I had a tough time starting a conversation and was socially awkward; I didn't talk too much. I shared too much when I was younger, depending on my personality.

36. On a scale of one to ten, with ten being easiest, how easy is it for you to start a conversation with a stranger? Three

37. On a scale of one to ten, with ten being easiest, how easy is it for you to network with others in the workplace? Five

38. What are some tools you use to maintain relationships with others? Phone, email, text, social media

39. What is your preferred method of communication (email, in person, phone, and so forth)? In person

40. How much energy does it take for you to navigate the corporate or white-collar working environment? It has taken a lot of energy over my career; it doesn't require a lot of energy now.

Emotional Intelligence and Introversion/Extroversion Tendency Interview (40 Questions)

Send to Dr. Reginald Ramsey, PhD, MBA, CISA, @ HRTC1906@ gmail.com

Name:__Male/White/Executive_____

Response Date: __5/18/2022_____

1. What is your official job title? Divisional chief, US government agency. I'm a first-line executive.

2. How long have you been in your current role? Four years

3. What attributes or skills helped you to reach your current career level? Persistence, resilience, job knowledge, on-the-job training, education, and professional experience

4. What does your typical day entail? Please elaborate as much as possible. Composing, mentoring. I have seven senior managers, two others. I've learned not to micromanage; I work across agencies.

5. How many hours do you work per week? Fifty

6. What advice would you give to someone who wants to be in your position someday? Learn as much as you can. Create an environment of trust. Learn about emotional intelligence development and adaptative management. Learn not to be rigid; be openminded. Use a bottom-up approach. Listen to people in the field, create an ownership environment, and risk tolerance for failure. Look for teaching moments.

7. What has been the role of mentors or coaches in your career advancement? I don't have a good mentoring program beyond my buddies. I created a mentoring program.

8. How many mentors do you have or have had over your career? Three long-term mentors, seven mentors over thirty-two years

9. How often do you speak or communicate with your mentor or mentors? It varies; sometimes it's once per month. Sometimes it's daily.

10. How do you balance your work with your private life? I was married to the job, an overachiever. Now I make time for my family. I set goals daily and weekly. I prioritize better.

11. How often do you set goals? I work every year, quarterly, weekly.

12. What type of goals do you set (yearly, monthly, and so forth)? Professional goals

13. How long have you been working in the market space? Forty years

14. What was your first job? Paperboy. I was also a stocker at a drugstore.

15. What valuable lessons have you learned over your career? Give people second chances; it's all about the people.

16. What type of spiritual life do you have? Spiritual. I was raised Roman Catholic; I believe in a higher power.

17. Do you attend or engage in any religious activities? I go to church on the holidays and for baptisms.

18. What role has emotional intelligence played in your career progression? It helped me to master my work environment. "Don't count heads but make heads count." Everyone has development needs.

19. What are some unwritten rules or norms you learned from being in a white-collar environment? Don't compare your career path. Be careful on your ascent; the air gets thin. Be nice to people on the way up; treat everyone with respect. Don't be the gossiping person; that is very cutthroat. Instead of power by title, seek title by competence. Create political capital with social and technical goals; depend on change management.

20. Did your parents or grandparents work in a white-collar setting? Yes or no? No

21. Did your parents or grandparents teach you how to navigate a white-collar working environment? No. My father transitioned from blue to white collar.

22. What did your parents or grandparents teach you about working in a white-collar environment? Work hard; don't always raise your hand.

23. How did you learn about these unwritten rules or norms (observation, mentors, mistakes)? All of the above

24. Currently, how many individuals do you mentor? A lot

25. How often do you listen to or read about successful individuals? All the time

26. What role has self-talk played in your career success? Very little. Be prepared for an interview. Put a song on. Play music.

27. How do you motivate yourself each day? See my daughter; she motivates me.

28. What are some of your hobbies? Juju, singing, working out, cooking, reading

29. Do you believe in the PIE model for career success? Yes

30. How often do you exercise? Three times per week

31. How much time do you take off each year to recharge your batteries? Five weeks

32. May I use your name in the book? (Keep confidential.) NA

33. Whom would you recommend I interview for this book? NA

34. How would you characterize yourself (either introverted or extroverted)? Extroverted

35. What introverted or extroverted qualities do you daily display to the general public?

    I'm comfortable with different people; I do presentations.

36. On a scale of one to ten, with ten being easiest, how easy is it for you to start a conversation with a stranger? Eight to nine

37. On a scale of one to ten, with ten being easiest, how easy is it for you to network with others in the workplace? Nine

38. What are some tools you use to maintain relationships with others? Caring, following up, learning from my parents, showing empathy toward others, assessing needs

39. What is your preferred method of communication (email, in person, phone, and so forth)? It depends on the situation. I prefer text and in person.

40. How much energy does it take for you to navigate the corporate or white-collar working environment? A lot. There is a lot of politics in a cut-throat environment. Leading up is tough; managing up is exhausting.

Emotional Intelligence and Introversion/Extroversion Tendency Interview (40 Questions)

Send to Dr. Reginald Ramsey, PhD, MBA, CISA, @ <u>HRTC1906@</u> <u>gmail.com</u>

Name:____Male/Asian/Executive_____

Response Date: __5/6/2022_____

1. What is your official job title? EVP/CIDO. I'm a board members and advisory board member, three largest VC in the world BOD. I'm owner of my own VC and AI company (storage locker). I possess a digital Media PhD with my dissertation at Northeastern University. I will be doing my defense soon.

2. How long have you been in your current role? Two years

3. What attributes or skills helped you to reach your current career level? Two things: I'm very intellectually curious and connect unconnectable things. I find relationships. I am not in the technology business. I am in the people business. I love to mentor; I believe a company exists for its people.

4. What does your typical day entail? Please elaborate as much as possible. There is no typical day; I like that about my job. I keep Fridays meeting free. I do email maintenance, calls with others, and airport runs.

5. How many hours do you work per week? I don't count. Over seventy to eighty hours per week. I'm having fun.

6. What advice would you give to someone who wants to be in your position someday? Don't set a goal that is too specific. Have an idea and be free enough. Prepare for the goal. Keep volunteering. Don't limit yourself and don't allow others to limit you.

7. What has been the role of mentors or coaches in your career advancement? Everything. One was a Harvard professor. These days, a type of self-made man, if he thanks himself, only thanks himself. I have a lot of direct mentors and a lot of indirect mentors. People are willing to accept my call.

8. How many mentors do you have or have had over your career? Eight mentors or more

9. How often do you speak or communicate with your mentor or mentors? Very regularly. Less regularly. I travel a lot and like to catch up over dinner.

10. How do you balance your work with your private life? I've been married for twenty-seven years. My wife really understands me and works with me. We take a lot of vacations together. I give back to my wife and daughter.

11. How often do you set goals? All the time. I have a ten-year-old; I have short-term goals. Write your own obituary ... all the goals before you die.

12. What type of goals do you set (yearly, monthly, and so forth)? Ten-year goals

13. How long have you been working in the market space? Thirty years

14. What was your first job? Lab guy

15. What valuable lessons have you learned over your career? When things go wrong, it's not always your fault. It's always about people.

16. What type of spiritual life do you have? NA

17. Do you attend or engage in any religious activities? NA

18. What role has emotional intelligence played in your career progression? It's all about EI and people.

19. What are some unwritten rules or norms you learned from being in a white-collar environment? People value who can get along. Don't run to HR or legal. Safety is important; learn to shut up.

20. Did your parents or grandparents work in a white-collar setting? Yes or no? Yes

21. Did your parents or grandparents teach you how to navigate a white-collar working environment? Yes

22. What did your parents or grandparents teach you about working in a white-collar environment? I observed my dad; he networked with others.

23. How did you learn about these unwritten rules or norms (observation, mentors, mistakes)? Observation

24. Currently, how many individuals do you mentor? Eight

25. How often do you listen to or read about successful individuals? Regularly. I listen to the *Waxman Report* now.

26. What role has self-talk played in your career success?

27. How do you motivate yourself each day? First, I have goals. How many people are depending on me?

28. What are some of your hobbies? Traveling, reading

29. Do you believe in the PIE model for career success?

30. How often do you exercise? Ten thousand steps per day. I run sometimes.

31. How much time do you take off each year to recharge your batteries? Traveling

32. May I use your name in the book? Keep confidential.

33. Whom would you recommend I interview for this book?

34. How would you characterize yourself (either introverted or extroverted)? Introverted

35. What introverted or extroverted qualities do you daily display to the general public? No one believes me. I interact with people all the time. I am a recovering introvert.

36. On a scale of one to ten, with ten being easiest, how easy is it for you to start a conversation with a stranger? One or two

37. On a scale of one to ten, with ten being easiest, how easy is it for you to network with others in the workplace? Ten

38. What are some tools you use to maintain relationships with others? I reach out through text messages while on a plane or through lunch and dinner.

39. What is your preferred method of communication (email, in person, phone, and so forth)? Phone and text; email is the worst.

40. How much energy does it take for you to navigate the corporate or white-collar working environment? There is a lot of political stuff. It takes a lot of energy.

Emotional Intelligence and Introversion/Extroversion Tendency Interview (40 Questions)

Send to Dr. Reginald Ramsey, PhD, MBA, CISA, @ HRTC1906@ gmail.com

Name:___Female/Middle Eastern/Executive_____

Response Date: __5/12/2022_____

1. What is your official job title? President, Private Midwestern University

2. How long have you been in your current role? Seven years

3. What attributes or skills helped you to reach your current career level? Effective leadership, perseverance, tenacity, being thick skinned, high levels of emotional intelligence, self-awareness, building professional relationships, asking for help, connections with a social network, and overcoming shyness tendencies

4. What does your typical day entail? Please elaborate as much as possible. Meetings. During these meetings, I ask for $1 million to $10 million. I make decisions. I spend time with students. Nearly one to two times per week, I interact with students.

5. How many hours do you work per week? Approximately sixty

6. What advice would you give to someone who wants to be in your position someday? Go for it! Work your way backward to the position; identify your gaps and fill them. Surround yourself with people who encourage you.

7. What has been the role of mentors or coaches in your career advancement? Mentors—I had to seek out a very important

person. Both mentors served to be honest and helped me to identify my strengths.

8. How many mentors do you have or have had over your career? Four formal mentors

9. How often do you speak or communicate with your mentor or mentors? Monthly

10. How do you balance your work with your private life? Not well. I'm horrible at this. I belong to a small network of women presidents. I build in self-care, exercise, and a spiritual time.

11. How often do you set goals? Yearly and weekly

12. What type of goals do you set (yearly, monthly, and so forth)? Work and personal

13. How long have you been working in the market space? Thirty-four years

14. What was your first job? Territory sales manager

15. What valuable lessons have you learned over your career? Don't sweat the small stuff. This too shall pass. Pick your battles.

16. What type of spiritual life do you have? I'm very spiritual. It's a big part of my life.

17. Do you attend or engage in any religious activities? Yes

18. What role has emotional intelligence played in your career progression? A huge role

19. What are some unwritten rules or norms you learned from being in a white-collar environment? Don't get upset with stereotyping.

I thought my husband, not me, was the president at various events. Controlling your emotions is important.

20. Did your parents or grandparents work in a white-collar setting? Yes or no? My parents worked in a white-collar setting; my grandparents were blue-collar workers.

21. Did your parents or grandparents teach you how to navigate a white-collar working environment? No

22. What did your parents or grandparents teach you about working in a white-collar environment? Work hard; family is important.

23. How did you learn about these unwritten rules or norms (observation, mentors, mistakes)? All of the above

24. Currently, how many individuals do you mentor? Five

25. How often do you listen to or read about successful individuals? Every day. I listen to podcasts and read about positive things daily.

26. What role has self-talk played in your career success? A huge role. It is very powerful.

27. How do you motivate yourself each day? I have a mindset shift ... I've got to make it happen.

28. What are some of your hobbies? Jogging, exercising, walking, reading, sitting in the sun next to the water, spending time with family, and traveling

29. Do you believe in the PIE model for career success? No

30. How often do you exercise? Five to six days per week

31. How much time do you take off each year to recharge your batteries? Three weeks to one month per year

32. May I use your name in the book? NA

33. Whom would you recommend I interview for this book? NA

34. How would you characterize yourself (either introverted or extroverted)? Extroverted. However, I'm moving closer to introversion as I get older.

35. What introverted or extroverted qualities do you daily display to the general public? Introverted. I think before I speak; I listen well.

36. On a scale of one to ten, with ten being easiest, how easy is it for you to start a conversation with a stranger? Ten

37. On a scale of one to ten, with ten being easiest, how easy is it for you to network with others in the workplace? Nine

38. What are some tools you use to maintain relationships with others? LinkedIn. I don't like the phone. I also like FaceTime, notes, and text messages.

39. What is your preferred method of communication (email, in person, phone, and so forth)? In person

40. How much energy does it take for you to navigate the corporate or white-collar working environment? A lot of energy

Emotional Intelligence and Introversion/Extroversion Tendency Interview (40 Questions)

Send to Dr. Reginald Ramsey, PhD, MBA, CISA, @ HRTC1906@ gmail.com

Name:__Black/Male/Executive_ _____

Dr. Reginald L. Ramsey, PhD, MBA, CISA

Response Date: ___7/17/2022_____

1. What is your official job title? Assistant vice president

2. How long have you been in your current role? Two years

3. What attributes or skills helped you to reach your current career level? Written and verbal communications skills, Microsoft Word, Excel, and business knowledge

4. What does your typical day entail? Please elaborate as much as possible. I underwrite real estate transactions and have meetings.

5. How many hours do you work per week? Forty-five

6. What advice would you give to someone who wants to be in your position someday? Develop strong communication skills; you won't know all the answers, but you know who to call for answers.

7. What has been the role of mentors or coaches in your career advancement? I did both mentoring and coaching of younger and older guys. I copied people I watched. I had one theme: "We do what we say we are going to do." I can't always do it. This message has helped me a lot.

8. How many mentors do you have or have had over your career? Three to five

9. How often do you speak or communicate with your mentor or mentors? Daily

10. How do you balance your work with your private life? I stay as long as it takes (8 or 9 p.m. sometimes). I work Saturday or Sunday from time to time. Work is work; my private life is my private life.

11. How often do you set goals? I have annual work-related goals. Personal goals are set loosely. I have a "honey-do" list.

12. What type of goals do you set (yearly, monthly, and so forth)? Annually

13. How long have you been working in the market space? Thirty-four years

14. What was your first job? Paperboy when I was eight or nine years old. This helped to develop patterns of discipline.

15. What valuable lessons have you learned over your career? Your reputation means a lot. You can dress or speak well, but you need a good reputation. Do what you say you are going to do.

16. What type of spiritual life do you have? I start with prayer. I joined a church in 1999; it helped me to deal with the vicissitudes of life.

17. Do you attend or engage in any religious activities? Yes

18. What role has emotional intelligence played in your career progression? It helps me control my emotions and evaluate the emotions of others. It helps to show vulnerability; my spiritual life has helped me. With experience I have learned to control my emotions.

19. What are some unwritten rules or norms you learned from being in a white-collar environment? I like to drink a lot. I can talk one way at work but talk differently at home. I use two languages; I need to stay professional.

20. Did your parents or grandparents work in a white-collar setting? Yes or no? No

21. Did your parents or grandparents teach you how to navigate a white-collar working environment? No

22. What did your parents or grandparents teach you about working in a white-collar environment?

23. How did you learn about these unwritten rules or norms (observation, mentors, mistakes)? Observations

24. Currently, how many individuals do you mentor? Two

25. How often do you listen to or read about successful individuals? Infrequently

26. What role has self-talk played in your career success? It is very important.

27. How do you motivate yourself each day? Morning prayers; I ask to be productive. Prayer has played a big role.

28. What are some of your hobbies? Golf, puzzles in the papers, and mind teasers. Puzzles help me in my job; I do all types of puzzles.

29. Do you believe in the PIE model for career success? It makes sense to me. Networking is a flaw of mine. I am introverted.

30. How often do you exercise? I walk the golf course.

31. How much time do you take off each year to recharge your batteries? Six weeks of vacation but only 2.5 weeks per year

32. May I use your name in the book? NA

33. Whom would you recommend I interview for this book?

34. How would you characterize yourself (either introverted or extroverted)? Introverted

35. What introverted or extroverted qualities do you daily display to the general public?

I am kind, but I mind my business.

36. On a scale of one to ten, with ten being easiest, how easy is it for you to start a conversation with a stranger? Six

37. On a scale of one to ten, with ten being easiest, how easy is it for you to network with others in the workplace? Six to seven

38. What are some tools you use to maintain relationships with others? Respect their discipline; remember past successes.

39. What is your preferred method of communication (email, in person, phone, and so forth)? Phone

40. How much energy does it take for you to navigate the corporate or white-collar working environment? It's not too hard.

Emotional Intelligence and Introversion/Extroversion Tendency Interview (40 Questions)

Send to Dr. Reginald Ramsey, PhD, MBA, CISA, @ HRTC1906@ gmail.com

Name:___White/Female/Executive_____

Response Date: ___6/27/2022_____

1. What is your official job title? Data management executive

2. How long have you been in your current role? Three years

3. What attributes or skills helped you to reach your current career level? Having a high interest level in my subject matter, doing

strategic thinking, looking beyond the problem at hand, seeing the broader picture, never assuming I was the smartest person in the room, solving problems with smart people, being good at pulling the best from people, and having servant leadership

4. What does your typical day entail? Please elaborate as much as possible. I found the right balance between listening and talking, providing and receiving feedback. Let people get to their conclusions; don't overtalk.

5. How many hours do you work per week? I drove to retirement, working fifty-five to sixty-five hours per week. I would not add more people; HR wouldn't allow more people.

6. What advice would you give to someone who wants to be in your position someday? Be a subject matter expert but don't be completely bound to it. Be open to trying new opportunities.

7. What has been the role of mentors or coaches in your career advancement? Earlier in my career, I didn't have a mentor. I had a great first manager; he mentored me. Find someone who "gets you." Find someone who will not judge you. Ask for a good mentor.

8. How many mentors do you have or have had over your career? Over a forty-year career, I've had eight to ten mentors. I always have one mentor; you may need to split up mentor responsibilities.

9. How often do you speak or communicate with your mentor or mentors? It depended on the situation. I got in touch regularly once per quarter to touch base. If I needed help, the connection was daily or weekly, just two minutes of advice. People asked for mentoring from me. I asked how often they needed to meet; sometimes it was once per month. I asked to schedule ad hoc meetings with their mentor.

10. How do you balance your work with your private life? I was bad at it; I had to define the boundaries.

11. How often do you set goals? This is not my strong suit. I envied people who did it. I was forced to stop and think about my goals annually. I worked with my mentor to pursue goals.

12. What type of goals do you set (yearly, monthly, and so forth)? Team goals, project goals, work goals, and personal goals. What are your gaps? What do you need from your management team? What happens if it can't be achieved?

13. How long have you been working in the market space? Forty years

14. What was your first job? Data analyst for the city of Indianapolis, Department of Metropolitan Development

15. What valuable lessons have you learned over your career? Surround yourself with smart people. Share your gifts. Be patient. Be open to new things. You will survive bad supervision but keep it as short as you can. Be your own advocate.

16. What type of spiritual life do you have? I have strong faith but little interest in organized religion.

17. Do you attend or engage in any religious activities? Not anymore

18. What role has emotional intelligence played in your career progression? I think it has been the key to all the success I had. I worked in IT, where emotional intelligence wasn't prevalent. I would say mine is higher than average; it really made me stand out as a supervisor. Anyone could surpass my technical skills, but he or she rarely exceeded my EQ.

19. What are some unwritten rules or norms you learned from being in a white-collar environment? Left unchecked, people will promote people who look and sound like them. The "rules" are different across genders, races, and so forth—it's not fair, and companies suffer as a result, but it will be a reality as long as the bulk of the people at the top are white and male.

20. Did your parents or grandparents work in a white-collar setting? Yes or no? Yes

21. Did your parents or grandparents teach you how to navigate a white-collar working environment? No

22. What did your parents or grandparents teach you about working in a white-collar environment? Nothing. I don't remember a single piece of work advice from either of them. Isn't that weird? Either I've forgotten all they said, or they just thought it was better if I figured it out for myself. Of course, my dad died when I was twenty-three, so maybe he just hadn't gotten to the advice part yet.

23. How did you learn about these unwritten rules or norms (observation, mentors, mistakes)? Painful observation mostly. Mentors were helpful, but since they were almost always male, they couldn't really see the world from my seat.

24. Currently, how many individuals do you mentor? I am open to talking to anyone, but I try to keep formal mentoring relationships to two to three so everyone gets the time he or she needs.

25. How often do you listen to or read about successful individuals? Daily

26. What role has self-talk played in your career success? I wish I had known what it was early in my career. I think it would have

helped with self-confidence and reduced frustration with career barriers.

27. How do you motivate yourself each day? Badly

28. What are some of your hobbies? Volunteer work, reading, and babysitting grandchildren

29. Do you believe in the PIE model for career success???

30. How often do you exercise? Not enough—three to four times a week when I'm good

31. How much time do you take off each year to recharge your batteries? One two-week vacation, a few short holidays

32. May I use your name in the book? If you really need to, but I'd prefer to be anonymous.

33. Whom would you recommend I interview for this book? People younger than I!

34. How would you characterize yourself (either introverted or extroverted)? Introverted

35. What introverted or extroverted qualities do you daily display to the general public? I usually test as an extrovert, but people would be surprised to know I hate being the center of attention, and I have to push myself to talk to strangers.

36. On a scale of one to ten, with ten being easiest, how easy is it for you to start a conversation with a stranger? Three

37. On a scale of one to ten, with ten being easiest, how easy is it for you to network with others in the workplace? Eight

38. What are some tools you use to maintain relationships with others? I'll talk to anyone who initiates the conversation with me. If you wait on me to schedule the discussion, you'll wait a long time.

39. What is your preferred method of communication (email, in person, phone, and so forth)? In person. For whatever reason, I hate the phone.

40. How much energy does it take for you to navigate the corporate or white-collar working environment? It got easier as I reached the end of my career—I really didn't have anything to lose. Also, once I realized I wasn't very willing to adapt to what my bosses thought I should be, things actually got easier—no more guilt over not adapting.

Emotional Intelligence and Introversion/Extroversion Tendency Interview (40 Questions)

Send to Dr. Reginald Ramsey, PhD, MBA, CISA, @ HRTC1906@ gmail.com

Name:__Black/Male/Executive_ _____

Response Date: _____6/27/2022_____

1. What is your official job title? Founder/president, nonprofit executive, and founding president of O.D. Johnson, LLC

2. How long have you been in your current role? Five years

3. What attributes or skills helped you to reach your current career level? Having a master's degree in public administration and being a servant leader. I'm open to debate, welcome challenges,

and used different types of leadership approach. I made crucial conversations.

4. What does your typical day entail? Please elaborate as much as possible. Speaking with people, researching particular duties, and executing the plan

5. How many hours do you work per week? Fifty-plus hours

6. What advice would you give to someone who wants to be in your position someday? Find an organization where you believe in the mission/vision and put people first.

7. What has been the role of mentors or coaches in your career advancement? I feel confident in saying that without the support of mentors, I wouldn't be where I am in life. I like bouncing ideas off these individuals and being pushed and challenged by these individuals to give my best.

8. How many mentors do you have or have had over your career? Many

9. How often do you speak or communicate with your mentor or mentors? Monthly

10. How do you balance your work with your private life? I've always tried to put my family first by attending events during and/or after school. I tried to rise early to get started with my day, and sometimes work required me to stay late. It was a struggle for me. (My family could better answer this question.)

11. How often do you set goals? It often depends on the project.

12. What type of goals do you set (yearly, monthly, and so forth)? Monthly

13. How long have you been working in the market space? Thirty-plus years

14. What was your first job? Shoe salesman at Dunham's Sports in August of 1990

15. What valuable lessons have you learned over your career? Serve people and treat them with respect.

16. What type of spiritual life do you have? I'm very much a person of faith.

17. Do you attend or engage in any religious activities? Yes! Regularly.

18. What role has emotional intelligence played in your career progression? As an African American man in the marketplace, operating in EI has kept me from many pitfalls.

19. What are some unwritten rules or norms you learned from being in a white-collar environment? Stay in my lane.

20. Did your parents or grandparents work in a white-collar setting? Yes and no. My mom worked in a white-collar setting. My dad worked in a blue-collar setting.

21. Did your parents or grandparents teach you how to navigate a white-collar working environment? Somewhat

22. What did your parents or grandparents teach you about working in a white-collar environment? We had conversations about race, hard work, and how to walk in integrity.

23. How did you learn about these unwritten rules or norms (observation, mentors, mistakes)? Parents, family, and mentors

24. Currently, how many individuals do you mentor? Too many to name

25. How often do you listen to or read about successful individuals? Frequently

26. What role has self-talk played in your career success? It's my gifting.

27. How do you motivate yourself each day? Prayer, music, reading, and learning from others

28. What are some of your hobbies? Exercise, reading, dancing, travel

29. Do you believe in the PIE model for career success? NA

30. How often do you exercise? Daily

31. How much time do you take off each year to recharge your batteries? A week or so, a lot of mini vacations

32. May I use your name in the book? Yes

33. Whom would you recommend I interview for this book? A former state representative

34. How would you characterize yourself (either introverted or extroverted)? Depending on the setting, both. I'm mostly extroverted.

35. What introverted or extroverted qualities do you daily display to the general public? Introverted

36. On a scale of one to ten, with ten being easiest, how easy is it for you to start a conversation with a stranger? Ten

37. On a scale of one to ten, with ten being easiest, how easy is it for you to network with others in the workplace? Seven to eight

38. What are some tools you use to maintain relationships with others? Phone

39. What is your preferred method of communication (email, in person, phone, and so forth)? In person

40. How much energy does it take for you to navigate the corporate or white-collar working environment? Not much

CHAPTER 8

EMOTIONAL INTELLIGENCE

Global employers have long been calling for higher levels of personal and interpersonal skills among the college graduates they hire (Porter and McKibbin 1988). Global companies are looking for creative means to grow and stay profitable. Gostick and Elton (2007) indicated that there is a need to develop and utilize every employee to his or her full potential without losing the high-potential employees. Global companies are looking for innovative means to achieve this worthy goal. There are obstacles that may thwart this goal for some individuals. The importance of developing each employee regardless of his or her background, culture, national origin, ethnicity, and gender is vitally important to the success of any global corporation.

Goleman (1995) indicated that emotional intelligence might play a role in developing personal and interpersonal skills. Goleman (1995) defined emotional intelligence as the ability to recognize and understand emotions and the skill to use this awareness to manage oneself and one's associations with others. Emotional intelligence consists of five components: knowing one's emotions, managing emotions, motivating oneself, recognizing emotions in other people, and handling associations (Goleman 1995).

Emotional intelligence has been investigated in several recent studies. Schumacher, Wheeler, and Carr (2009) studied the association between emotional intelligence and buyers' performance.

They found that buyers' emotional intelligence is positively related to association performance, most significantly from the perspective of their key suppliers. Depape et al. (2006) researched the association of emotional intelligence and self-talk on Canadian university students. Self-talk has been discussed in the literature as a means of enhancing self-awareness and self-regulation, both of which are considered important in the construct of emotional intelligence. Depape et al. (2006) found significant positive relations between emotional intelligence and self-talk. Yarrish and Law (2009) explored the difference in the emotional intelligence of first-year business students. Yarrish and Law (2009) found that students need increased emotional intelligence development in all areas. In addition, research by Shipley, Jackson, and Segrest (2010) posited the effects of emotional intelligence on age, work experience, and academic performance. Shipley, Jackson, and Segrest (2010) found that age was not positively correlated with emotional intelligence. However, work experience and academic performance were (Shipley et al. 2010).

Emotional intelligence, in laymen's terms, can be thought of as how one relates to and gets along with other people. In other words, it's how you build and maintain relations with other people. Some people are very good at making and maintaining friends. However, some people are not. In the white-collar business environment, it's important to be able to build and maintain friendships, especially with those in positions of power and authority.

Emotional Intelligence Defined

Research on emotional intelligence (EI) began as early as the 1930s with researchers Thorndike and Stein (1937) and Wechsler (1943). Wechsler (1958) defined *intelligence* as the global capacity of an individual or person to act purposefully, to think rationally, and to work harmoniously and congruently with his or her environment. Wechsler (1943) posited that total intelligence cannot be measured without some level of nonintellectual factors being included. Gardner (1983) wrote about multiple intelligences and proposed that intrapersonal and interpersonal intelligence are as important as the type of intelligence typically measured by traditional intelligence (IQ) and related tests (Webb 2009).

Salovey and Mayer (1990, 189) indicated that emotional intelligence included an "ability to monitor one's own and others' feelings and emotions, to discriminate among them and to use this information to guide one's thinking and actions." Emotional intelligence has been defined as the "ability to adaptively recognize emotion, express emotion, regulate emotion, and harness emotions" (Schutte et al. 1998, 37).

Building on the research of Salovey, Mayer, and Goleman, I would like to offer this emotional intelligence (EI) development model:

Proposed Emotional Intelligence (EI) Development Model

Self-Awareness	Development Methods/Tools	Assessment Methods
Emotional self-awareness Accurate self-assessment Self-confidence	360-degree feedback questionnaire Self-awareness survey (pre/post) Learning contracts Self-awareness courses/ workshops Mentors/coaches Accountability partner EI survey (pre/post)	360-degree feedback results Personal observations Self-awareness course scores Personal interviews EI survey results
Self-Management Emotional self-control Transparency Adaptability Achievement Initiative Optimism	**Development Methods/Tools** 360-degree feedback questionnaire Self-management courses/ workshops Facilitated role-playing exercises Learning contracts (Knowles 1975) Mentors/coaches Accountability partner EI survey (pre/post)	**Assessment Methods** 360-degree feedback results Self-management course scores Personal observations Personal interviews EI survey results

Social Awareness	Development Methods/Tools	Assessment Methods
Empathy Organizational awareness Service	360-degree feedback questionnaire EI survey (pre/post) Social awareness courses/ workshops Learning contracts (Knowles 1975) Intentional change theory model (Boyatzis 2006) interviews (pre/post)	360-degree feedback results EI survey results Social awareness course scores Learning contracts observation Personal observations Personal interviews
Relationship Management	Development Methods/Tools	Assessment Methods
Inspirational leadership Influence Developing others Change catalyst Conflict management Building bonds Teamwork/ collaboration	360-degree feedback questionnaire Leadership development courses Conflict management courses Role-playing exercises EI survey (pre/post) Relationship management courses	360-degree feedback results Leadership development course scores EI survey results Conflict management course scores Personal observations Interviews (pre/post)

Proposed Emotional Intelligence (EI) Development Model

Based on the emotional intelligence literature and the analysis of this research, this researcher proposes the emotional intelligence development model to help facilitate the development of emotional intelligence from the primary (K–12) school to the higher education levels. This proposed emotional intelligence development model should be used in conjunction with traditional or cognitive intelligence development curricula. The cost for this proposed emotional intelligence development model may be funded from private dollars in the initial stages. However, as the program grows and expands, the expenses and costs may be allocated from current public school budgets. In addition, some of the funding would have to come from state and federal government sources.

In today's US educational system, the primary focus has centered on cognitive or traditional intelligence. There seems to be a consensus around the fact that cognitive intelligence or abilities increase one's capacity to learn and process relevant information more rapidly and accurately (Fulmer and Barry 2004). The results of hundreds of studies revealed two generalizations regarding cognitive intelligence. First, cognitive intelligence is predictive of individual outcomes in a wide variety of settings (e.g., educational success, occupational training success, job performance, decision-making performance, health, and social outcomes (Gottfredson 2004). Second, cognitive intelligence provides greater practical advantages in novel or complex settings than in simpler situations (Gottfredson 1997). Higher cognitive intelligence abilities predict better decision-making performance (LePine, Colquitt, and Erez 2000). Cognitive intelligence abilities enable an individual to "reason, plan, solve problems, think abstractly, comprehend complex ideas, learn quickly, and learn from experience" (Gottfredson 1997, 13). Hunter (1986) noted that cognitive intelligence abilities are related to performance itself, not just to job or subject knowledge. Highly and cognitively intelligent individuals are faster at cognitive operations on the job or in school settings. These highly cognitively intelligent individuals are better able to prioritize conflicting rules and to adapt old procedures to alter current situations.

With the need to develop students' emotional and social competencies, this researcher proposes that the emotional intelligence development model may be used as a tool for administrators and school officials. This model is based on the framework by Goleman et al. (2002). This proposed model is called the "emotional intelligence (EI) development model." The model addresses four primary emotional intelligence domains with their associated competencies. The four domains are self-awareness, self-management, social awareness, and relationship management (Goleman et al. 2002). This model provides a simple approach for emotional intelligence development, along with tools and methods to improve emotional intelligence competencies. In addition, it offers a means of assessment.

The assessment tools may be modified on an as-needed basis. However, the proposed emotional intelligence development model provides a framework that could be the genesis and catalyst for policy makers, lawmakers, school administrators, and school officials to develop the emotional and social competencies of today's US-based students.

The proposed emotional intelligence development model is adapted from the emotional intelligence domains and competencies of Goleman et al. (2002). The development methods and tools are very practical and reasonable. In addition, the assessment methods are simple yet very helpful in ascertaining valuable and useful data points to improve student outcomes. The emotional intelligence development models found there were adapted from Goleman et al. (2002).

Self-Awareness

Goleman et al. (2002) indicated that self-awareness included three personal competencies: (1) emotional self-awareness, (2) accurate self-assessment, and (3) self-confidence. Self-awareness is the ability to honestly reflect on and understand one's emotions, strengths, challenges, motives, values, goals, and dreams. One is able to see the big picture in a complex situation. Self-awareness helps an individual to be candid and authentic, which allows him or her to speak and express himself or herself in an open, clear manner with emotions and conviction.

Self-awareness provides the primary building block for the other three domains (self-management, social awareness, and relationship management). An individual who cannot adequately know and understand himself or herself would have a difficult time trying to manage his or her own emotions, assess the emotions of others, and use that information to manage relationships with others (Goleman et al. 2002). Emotional self-awareness is the ability to read one's own emotions and recognize their impact using one's inner signals to guide one's decisions (Goleman et al. 2002). Accurate self-assessment is the ability to know and understand one's strengths and limitations. In addition, one is able to exhibit a sense of humor about them. One is able to have gracefulness in learning in the areas in which one needs to improve. In essence, one is able to accept and welcome constructive criticism and feedback.

Self-confidence is defined as a sound sense of one's self-worth and capabilities. It allows an individual to have a sense of presence and self-assurance that allows him or her to stand out in a group (Goleman et al. 2002).

Self-Management

Self-management has six personal competencies: (1) self-control, (2) transparency, (3) adaptability, (4) achievement, (5) initiative, and (6) optimism. Goleman et al. (2002) noted that self-management is equated to an ongoing inner conversation and "is the component of emotional intelligence that frees us from being a prisoner of our feelings. It is what allows the mental clarity and concentrated energy that leadership demands and what keeps disruptive emotions from throwing us off track" (46). It is difficult to achieve one's personal goals and aspirations without effective self-management. Managing one's emotions and being open to others about one's feelings, beliefs, and actions help to establish trust, integrity, and personal capital (Goleman et al. 2002).

Self-control is defined as the ability to manage disturbing emotions and impulses and to channel them in a useful way. Self-control enables one to stay calm and clearheaded under high stress or during a crisis (Goleman et. al. 2002). Transparency is the ability to display one's feelings, beliefs, and actions. This allows for integrity. Transparency helps one to openly admit mistakes or faults. In addition, transparency emboldens one to confront unethical behavior in others rather than to turn a blind eye (Goleman et al. 2002).

Adaptability allows one to juggle multiple demands and priorities without losing one's focus or energy. It enables one to feel comfortable with ambiguities and difficult life situations and helps one to be flexible, nimble, and limber in the face of new challenges in life (Goleman et al. 2002). Adaptability facilitates one's ability to overcome many of life's obstacles (Goleman et al. 2002).

Achievement drives an individual to have high personal standards, which drives him or her to constantly seek performance improvements. It helps one to be pragmatic and honest about one's goals and career intentions, and enables one to set challenging goals that are measurable and attainable. Achievement pushes one to continually learn and grow (Goleman et al. 2002).

Initiative is the ability of one to act and seize opportunities. It allows one to create better possibilities for himself or herself and others, and it enables one to take control of one's own career intentions and destiny.

Optimism is seeing an opportunity rather than a threat in a major setback or difficulty. It allows one to positively look for the best in others. Optimism is expecting better days and outcomes in the future.

Social Awareness

Social awareness is composed of three social competencies: (1) empathy, (2) organizational awareness, and (3) service. Social awareness is defined as having the quality of being acutely aware of the emotions and needs of others. Goleman et al. (2002) indicated the following: "By being attuned to how others feel in the moment, a leader can say and do what's appropriate—whether it be to calm fears, assuage anger, or join in good spirits. This attunement also lets a leader sense the shared values and priorities that can guide the group" (49).

In essence, social awareness enables an individual to monitor and adjust strategy and direction, and work toward accomplishing a shared vision. It helps an individual or leader to know when to push and capitalize on the momentum of the group and when to pull back and encourage reflection and collective reexamination of the purpose and priorities (Goleman et al. 2002).

Empathy is the ability to be attuned to a wide range of emotional signals that let one sense others' emotions. It helps one to understand others' perspectives and beliefs. Empathy helps one to get along with other people of diverse backgrounds and different cultures, and allows one to listen very carefully to others and grasp their perspectives or opinions. Organizational awareness allows one to be attuned to organizational norms. Organizational awareness helps one to navigate and operate effectively in an environment with political and social networks and relationships. It helps one to be aware of the guiding values and unspoken rules that need to be adhered to and followed (Goleman et al. 2002).

Service fosters an emotional climate that allows one to keep relationships on the right track. It enables one to monitor and adjust to others' needs. Service helps one to stay attuned and attentive to others' desires (Goleman et al. 2002).

Relationship Management

Relationship management includes six social competencies: (1) inspiration, (2) influence, (3) the development of others, (4) change catalyst, (5) conflict management, and (6) teamwork and collaboration.

Relationship management germinates from the domains of self-awareness, self-management, and social awareness, allowing the emotionally intelligent individual to effectively manage emotions perceived in others. It allows one to cultivate webs of relationships, find common ground, and use shared vision to motivate people to move forward toward accomplishing a mission or goal (Goleman et al. 2002).

Inspiration allows one to create resonance and motivates others to follow.

Resonance means people's emotional centers are in sync in a positive way (Goleman et al. 2002).

Inspiration enables one to be a positive example to others. It helps one to articulate a shared mission and compelling vision that inspires others to follow (Goleman et al. 2002).

Influence helps one to find the right words that would appeal to others and helps him or her to get buy-in and acceptance from key individuals. It helps one to be persuasive and engaging when addressing a group or others.

Developing others means cultivating their abilities and competencies. It means showing a genuine interest in helping others to achieve their career intentions and life aspirations. It means understanding and appreciating others' goals, strengths, and weaknesses. It allows one to give timely and constructive feedback to others and to become a mentor or coach.

A change catalyst allows one to recognize the need for change and challenge the status quo. It helps one to become a strong advocate and proponent for positive change, even in the face of strong opposition or difficult circumstances, and to overcome barriers by finding practical and pragmatic solutions (Goleman et al. 2002).

Conflict management allows one to understand and appreciate all parties' sides and perspectives. It allows one to find a common and shared solution that would appeal to all parties and helps one to address a difficult situation with boldness and conviction of purpose (Goleman et al. 2002).

Teamwork and collaboration allow one to get along with others and enable one to create an atmosphere of friendly collegiality and respect for others. Teamwork and collaboration allow for respect, helpfulness, and cooperation among people on a team. They afford the opportunity to forge and create close relationships beyond just school or work obligations (Goleman et al. 2002).

In the emotional intelligence development model, the proposed development methods and tools include the following: a 360-degree feedback questionnaire, a self-awareness survey (pre/post), learning contracts, self-awareness courses and workshops, mentors and coaches, an accountability partner, and an emotional intelligence survey (pre/post). The 360-degree feedback questionnaire would help students understand how they are viewed from others' perspectives. This development method would be valuable to developing the students' sense of self-awareness and self-confidence. The student would have a genuine understanding of his or her competencies and abilities. When the student's behavioral weaknesses and strengths have been identified, a learning contract could be used to either systematically change or keep the student's behaviors.

The self-awareness survey would be given to students and their parents or guardians in the primary to high school grade levels. The students and their parents or guardians would be responsible for completing the self-awareness survey before the start of a school year. In addition, they would be responsible for completing the self-awareness survey after the school year. Each year, the students and the school administrators would be responsible for reviewing the self-awareness survey results in a private manner. The annual self-awareness reviews would build accountability into the process. The learning contracts would be used to develop a plan of action for the individual student. Each student would agree to a learning contract between the teachers, parents, and themselves. The learning contracts would be used in the primary to high school grade levels.

At the college level, first-year college students and their professors could use learning contracts. Self-awareness courses and workshops would serve to educate students on the essentials of self-awareness. These courses should be mandatory in the primary to high school levels. At the college level, self-awareness courses and workshops should be optional. Mentors and coaches should be identified and provided to any student from the primary to the college levels who wants one. The mentors and coaches would serve as role models

167

and examples. They would create a sense of community around the student.

The accountability partner could be a fellow student. He or she is responsible for ensuring that the student stays on track to achieve his or her goals.

The emotional intelligence survey (pre/post) should be used to identify which specific emotional intelligence competencies are strong and which are weak. Students should complete the emotional intelligence survey at the beginning and end of the academic school year. They should complete it in the primary to high school levels and in the first year of college or university.

In the proposed emotional intelligence development model, the following assessment methods should be used: 360-degree feedback results, personal observations, self-awareness courses scores, personal interviews, emotional intelligence survey results, self-management course scores, social awareness course scores, learning contract observation, leadership development course scores, and conflict management course scores. The 360-degree feedback results provide a barometer of how others perceive and view students. When these results are provided to students from the primary to the college levels, they give them a realistic view of how others perceive them. Students may use the feedback to modify and change their behavior. A trained behavior professional would administer the personal observations. The personal observations would serve as a means to monitor students' behavior in a safe and normal environment. Personal observations would be done voluntarily from the primary grades to the first year of college.

The self-awareness course scores would be used to identify how students are progressing. In addition, they would be able to observe their progress and determine which behaviors need to be changed or modified. Personal interviews would be done in conjunction with personal observations. The personal interviews would provide a qualitative research approach for identifying and developing students' behavioral needs. The personal interviews would be completed in a voluntary and confidential manner. The emotional intelligence survey results would serve as a vehicle to improve the emotional intelligence competencies of students from the primary to the first-year college level.

Students would be provided with their emotional intelligence survey results at the start and end of an academic school year. They would be able to track their emotional intelligence competence development. The self-management course and social awareness scores would be used to see whether students comprehend and understand the course material. The scores would be compiled and provided to students from the primary to the first-year college level. The learning contract observation would be used to see whether students have written down their learning contract. In addition, the learning observation would serve as a conversation starter between students and observers. If students need assistance with the learning contract, observers would direct them to the appropriate area. The leadership development course scores would serve to show whether students are grasping the primary leadership skills and competencies from the course material. The leadership development course and conflict management scores should be collected, compiled, and shared with students from the primary to the first year of college.

Research Questions

Research Question 1: What is the association between the emotional intelligence of first-year college students and their career intentions to complete their college degrees?

Research Question 2: What is the correlation between the emotional intelligence of first-year international college students and their career intentions to complete their college degrees?

Hypothesis H0[1] (Null Hypothesis): There will be no significant association between emotional intelligence (EIS) and first-year college students' career intentions to complete their degrees (CCI).

Hypothesis HA[1] (Alternative Hypothesis): There is a statistically positive association between emotional intelligence (EIS) and first-year college students' career intentions to complete their degree (CCI).

Hypothesis H0² (Null Hypothesis): There will be no significant difference between academic majors of study on emotional intelligence scores.

Hypothesis HA² (Alternative Hypothesis): There will be a significant difference between academic majors of study on emotional intelligence scores.

Conceptual/Theoretical Framework

For this study, the two theoretical frameworks that would be used are the Schutte et al. (1998) Emotional Intelligence Scale (EIS) and Larson et al.'s (1988) Coping with Career Indecision (CCI) scale. Schutte et al.'s (1998) Emotional Intelligence Scale (EIS) is a self-report measure that includes thirty-three items. In some literature, the Emotional Intelligence Scale is called the Assessing Emotions Scale. In addition, it is referred to as the Self-Report Emotional Intelligence Test or the Schutte Emotional Intelligence Scale (Schutte, Malouff, and Bhullar 2009).

To measure the ability of first-year college students' career intentions to cope with career indecision, a modified version of the Coping with Career Indecision (CCI) scale will be used (Larson et al. 1988).

CHAPTER 9

DEFINITIONS

This exploratory quantitative study will recruit and use only study participants from one Midwestern college for its sample set. Future research should incorporate a wider sample of participants. Future research should use a qualitative approach and more in-depth data to get more raw data from the study participants. In addition, future research needs to examine the association between emotional intelligence, work experience, and other individual-level variables, such as conscientiousness, that might have an important effect (Shipley, Jackson, and Segrest 2010).

Definition of Terms

- Baby boomers—American citizens born between the years 1946 and 1964 (Peters 2010)
- Community college—A two-year institution of higher learning. It meets the training needs of the sub-baccalaureate section of the workforce (Grubb et al. 2000).
- Coping with Career Indecision scale—A self-report measure that includes thirty-five items. It is commonly called CCI (Larson et al. 1988).
- Emotional Intelligence—The ability to recognize and understand emotions and the skill to use this awareness to

manage oneself and one's associations with others (Goleman 1995)

- Emotional Intelligence Scale—A self-report measure that includes thirty-three items. It is also called the "Assessing Emotional Scale" or the "Schutte Emotional Intelligence Scale" (Schutte, Malouff, and Bhullar 2009).
- Globalization—It is manifested in the freer and more large-scale mobility of capital and people between economies and societies, triggering political and cultural exchanges (Lasonen 2005).
- Nontraditional student—It includes individuals who haven't followed a continuous educational path into college (Newbold, Mehta, and Forbus 2010).
- Selected Control—It involves two defining processes. First, it refers to engaging in the pursuit of chosen goals and trying to change one's environment so goals can be achieved. Second, it refers to internal processes that enhance the motivation to pursue the goal by creating favorable representations of the goal and one's ability to pursue it (Schindler and Tomasik 2010).
- Self-leadership—It consists of a variety of interwoven strategies that address individuals' self-awareness, volition, motivation, cognition, and behavior (Manz and Neck 1991).
- Self-talk—The means of enhancing self-awareness and self-regulation, both of which are considered important in the construct of emotional intelligence (Depape at al. 2008).

Summary

Locke (1999) articulated that improving the economic and social conditions of a community or a particular group in the United States has always been linked to education. With the advances in technology and the globalization of society, postsecondary education or training is increasingly becoming a must. According to the Education Trust

(1999), state education CEOs investigating the gap between high school graduation and college or high-performance jobs stated, "Our nation is no longer well served by an education system that prepares a few to attend college to develop their minds for learned pursuits while the rest are expected only to build their muscles for useful labor. In the twenty-first century, all students must meet higher achievement standards in elementary, secondary, and postsecondary schools and thus be better prepared for the challenges of work and citizenship" (Locke 1999).

Success in today's global society demands that employees possess at least the skills and knowledge required of a high school graduate if they are to be competitive in the workforce of the twenty-first century and beyond. Failure to meet this minimum requirement, however, limits the economic and social potential of millions of young Americans each year (Hayes et al. 2002, US Department of Education 1999). The value of a college degree in a global society is very important to the community student. Therefore, this research will explore and examine the association between emotional intelligence and first-year college students' career intentions to complete their degrees. The data from this research will be shared with the academic community.

With the globalization of the workplace, it's imperative that everyone's voice is heard at the proverbial table. This includes those who may be depicted as introverted individuals. In most societies and cultures, the extroverted individual has been viewed as the leader. However, extroverted individuals can learn from their introverted colleagues. Introverted individuals are able to focus, think, reason, critically analyze, and help an organization to become wildly successful. How do I know this? I look at one of the companies where I invested over ten-plus years of life. That company's primary senior leaders and senior leadership team were composed of mostly introverted individuals. You may ask, "How do introverted individuals achieve such great success in the marketplace?" Throughout this book, let's explore this question.

This book was constructed with survey responses from several individuals with both blue-collar and white-collar backgrounds. You will notice that this survey data hasn't been edited or redacted. The author would like readers to come to their own conclusions based on the survey data provided. The author will attempt to reserve his opinion and conclusion in this book. Moreover, the reader is asked to think, reflect, and debate the author's assumptions and assertions. The author wants to truly understand what it takes to truly be successful in the eyes of each individual. The author understands that success can be viewed differently through the lens of each individual.

With the globalization of the workplace, it's imperative that everyone's voice is heard at the proverbial table. This includes individuals who may be depicted as introverted individuals or colleagues. In many societies and cultures, the extroverted individual has been viewed as the leader. However, extroverted individuals can learn from their introverted colleagues. Introverted individuals are able to focus, think, reason, critically analyze, and help an organization to become wildly successful. How do I know this? I look at one of the companies where I invested over ten-plus years of my life. That company's inner circle of senior leaders and the senior leadership team was composed of mostly introverted individuals. You may ask, "How do introverted individuals achieve such success?" Let's explore this question throughout this book.

This book shows the survey responses of several individuals. These individuals can be viewed as either introverted or extroverted. Based on the responses to the questions related to introversion and extroversion tendencies, the reader is able to deduce whether the respondent is an introverted or extroverted person. The reader will observe that these survey responses have not been edited or amplified by the author. The primary reason for this unedited version is to demonstrate with raw data how one can navigate through the corporate maze as either an introverted or extroverted individual. In some cases, it may be hard for the reader to figure out whether the respondent is an introverted or extroverted person. The author would like readers to come to their own conclusions based on the survey responses and the readers' interpretation of success. As we all know, success is an ephemeral phenomenon. Success is dependent on the individual's definition of success. In other words, success is an individual and personal experience, if you will.

Grant, Gino, and Hofmann (2014) posited, "In a dynamic, unpredictable environment, introverts are often more effective leaders, particularly when workers are proactive, offering ideas for improving the business." This may explain that when introverted leaders are managing proactive employees, they are much more likely to let those employees run with their ideas. They also show that though extroverted leaders play an important part in teams, they also "tend to command the center of attention and take over discussions" (Hofmann 2014).

Susan Cain (2012) also had some opinions on this issue, saying that extroverted leaders quite unwittingly get so excited about things that they put their own stamps on the team's work, and other people's ideas might not as easily be approved. This often leads to conflicts between leaders and employees, leading to a reduction in work performance.

You're going to find a what-if section in the book; so what if you didn't listen to that senior white lady who got on the plane next to you and indicated to you that she was going to commit suicide when she got home? What if you used your introverted tendencies and didn't listen to her? What if you also used your introverted tendencies and didn't listen to the college student who was suicidal? And what if you had to deal with that situation at a large university? What if you also tuned out the fact that other people came across your path who were suicidal, depressed, and couldn't find a way to cope, but you were too busy, too preoccupied? What were your priorities?

What if you were so loud and unapproachable that others didn't feel comfortable around you? What if people didn't trust you? So what if you were too introverted or extroverted and didn't listen to them? What if you didn't listen to a brother who had a heart transplant or a kidney transplant story to tell? What if you didn't listen to his story? What if you didn't listen to your cousin, who had brain cancer, kidney cancer, and throat cancer? What if you didn't take the time to sit and listen to his story? "What if" is an important question. Whether we are introverted and extroverted individuals, let's remember to use our kindness of humanity and listen to each other. Let's get out of our comfort zones, whether we be introverted or extroverted. Let's take the time to have some civility and listen to each other. We are our brothers' and sisters' keepers.

CHAPTER 10

LET'S REIMAGINE

Let's reimagine a global world. If a child is born in this big world and is black or white or Asian or Native American, that child gets the necessary encouragement and love. That child gets the necessary attention he or she needs to grow up, whether that child is born into a humble environment or a wealthy family environment. Let's imagine that this child gets what he or she needs to grow up and become a great leader. Let's imagine that little black child, who is born to a single mom or dad, is able to get the proper encouragement and coaching. That child is encouraged and expected to become great. Let's imagine that with the right mentoring and coaching, that child is able to grow up and become a Supreme Court justice or a vice president or president of the United States. Let's imagine that little white girl from humble beginnings who comes from Appalachia, Southern Indiana, or South Florida and is able to get the necessary encouragement and mentoring to become the secretary of state. Let's imagine that little white girl is able to become the president of the United States of America.

If you will, please imagine a world that is so different that all its citizens feel empowered, bold, and powerful. Can you imagine this new world? Let's imagine what it would be like if that Asian boy and girl were able to come from India, China, Korea, or Japan and were able to fully integrate into the American corporate and noncorporate environments. Let's imagine a world where each individual is respected and where we treat each other with respect and love. Let's imagine what it would be like to live in this beautiful and forgiving world. Now let's stop imagining, and let's go and make it happen. Let's be the change we want to see in this big world of ours! No excuses, just results. Let's just do it one person and one encounter at a time. We can do this.

Based on the survey responses and research, it appears that both introverted and extroverted individuals are prevalent in the global marketplace. Each individual has an individual story and experience. Introverted individuals must be willing to figure out a way to share or add their ideas and thoughts to the workplace conversation. Likewise, extroverted individuals must be willing to share the conversation space with their introverted colleagues. Why is this needed? In the global marketplace of ideas, all individuals' ideas are needed to compete and win in a global business environment.

Based on the evidence and the survey data I obtained through the various participants in the forty-question study I conducted, based on that small sample set, one of the things the author learned is that mentoring matters. It's impossible to be successful at a very high level, whether in a blue-collar or white-collar setting, without proper mentoring and coaching, so that's very important. One must obtain good mentors and coaches to help propel one forward in his or her career.

Mentoring is important. Without proper mentoring and coaching, one will have a very difficult time navigating a successful career that is either blue-collar or white-collar fields of employment. In addition, if one is unable to receive feedback, he or she will have a difficult time as well. One needs to be willing to accept both positive and constructive feedback to grow, develop, and become the best he or she can become. Success is a team endeavor. One cannot have great success without the engagement and socialization of others.

Likewise, we must be coachable to be successful in the global business environment. Coachability is extremely important to our success. In addition, our emotional intelligence must be developed to regulate our emotions. Emotional intelligence helps us to evaluate the emotions of others as well. It helps us to express empathy toward others and be able to motivate ourselves to move and be action oriented. We also learn to socialize and engage with others by developing our emotional intelligence. With the global nature of business, emotional intelligence development is essential to acquiring and keeping marketable and transferable job skills. These skills are highly sought after in a globally competitive business landscape.

Most successful people are able to communicate effectively. They are able to convey their thoughts to others in a clear, concise way; this allows them to be very clear about expectations of themselves and other people. This is such a tremendous asset to them, the power of communication, that it affords them freedom because now they are able to delegate tasks to others. Also, they recognize that life is a team sport; as such, they are able to navigate life better because they have a support team.

Some additional book themes I have observed are that one can be very successful as an introvert in a business setting. Also, one can develop success by developing his or her emotional intelligence. And one can navigate effectively, even if one is an introvert or extrovert. Let's continue this discussion. The author looks forward to hearing your thoughts, suggestions, and feedback. Please contact him, Dr. Reginald Ramsey, PhD, MBA, CISA, by emailing him at HRTC1906@gmail.com.

REFERENCES

Abraham, R. 2000. "The Role of Job Control as a Moderator of Emotional Dissonance and Emotional-Intelligence-Outcome Associations." *Journal of Psychology* 134: 169–184.

Adams, J., H. Khan, R. Raeside, and D. White. 2007. *Research Methods for Graduate Business and Social Science Students* (Los Angeles, CA: SAGE).

Akhtar, R., L. Boustani, D. Tsivrikos, and T. Chamorro-Premuzic. 2015. "The Engageable Personality: Personality and Trait EI as Predictors of Work Engagement." *Personality and Individual Differences* 73: 44–49.

Ang, S., and L. Van Dyne. 2008. "Conceptualization of Cultural Intelligence: Definition, Distinctiveness, and Nomological Network." *Handbook of Cultural Intelligence: Theory, Measurement, and Applications*: 3–15.

Arnett, J. 2004. *Emerging Adulthood: The Winding Road from the Late Teens through the Twenties*. New York: Oxford University Press.

Ashton, M.C., and Lee, K. 2009. "The HEXACO-60: A Short Measure of the Major Dimensions of Personality." *Journal of Personality Assessment* 91: 340–345.

Austin, E. 2004. "An Investigation of the Association between Traits of Emotional Intelligence and Emotional Task Performance." *Personality and Individual Differences* 36: 1855–64.

Austin, E., D. Saklofske, S. Huang, and D. McKenney. 2004. "Measurement of Trait of Emotional Intelligence: Testing and Cross-Validating a Modified Version of Schutte et al.'s (1998) Measure." *Personality and Individual Differences* 36: 555–562.

Azniza, I. 2005. "Different Effects of REBT Brief Group Intervention and Behavior Brief Group Intervention toward Maladjustment." Unpublished PhD diss., University Science, Malaysia.

Banta, T. W. 1993. *Making a Difference: Outcomes of a Decade of Assessment in Higher Education*. San Francisco: Jossey-Bass.

Bar-On, R. 2004. "The Bar-On Emotional Quotient Inventory (EQ-i): Rationale, Description, and Psychometric Properties." In *Measuring Emotional Intelligence: Common Ground and Controversy*, edited by G. Geher. Hauppauge, NY: Nova Science.

Barrick, M., and M. Mount. 1991. "The Big Five Personality Dimensions and Job Performance: A Meta-Analysis." *Personnel Psychology* 44: 1–26.

Bastian, V., N. Burns, and T. Nettelbeck. 2005. "Emotional Intelligence Predicts Life Skills, but Not as Well as Personality and Cognitive Abilities." *Personality and Individual Differences* 39: 1135–1145.

Bhati, K. 2022. "What Is Hyper-Independence? How to Overcome Hyper-Independence?" *Mental Disorders*.

Blevins, D., M. Stackhouse, and S. Dionne. 2022. "Righting the Balance: Understanding Introverts (and Extraverts) in the Workplace." *British Academy of Management* 24: 78–98.

Blustein, D. 1989. "The Role of Goal Instability and Career Self-Efficacy in the Career Exploration Process." *Journal of Vocational Behavior* 35: 194–203.

Bono, J. E., and T. A. Judge. 2004. "Personality and Transformational and Transactional Leadership: A Meta-Analysis." *Journal of Applied Psychology* 89 (5): 901–910.

Boyatzis, R. E. 1982. *The Competent Manager: A Model for Effective Performance*. New York: John Wiley & Sons.

Boyatzis, R. E. 2006. "Intentional Change Theory from a Complexity Perspective." *Journal of Management Development* 25: 607–623.

Boyatzis, R. E. 2009. "Competencies as a Behavioral Approach to Emotional Intelligence." *Journal of Management Development* 28: 749–70.

Boyatzis, R. E., A. Renio-McKee, and L. Thompson. 1995. *Past Accomplishments: Establishing the Impact and Baseline of Earlier Programs. Innovation in Professional Education: Steps on a Journey from Teaching to Learning*. San Francisco: Jossey-Bass.

Boyatzis, R., and A. Saatcioglu. 2008. "A 20-Year View of Trying to Develop Emotional, Social and Cognitive Intelligence Competencies in Graduate Management Education." *Journal of Management Development* 27: 92–108.

Boyatzis, R. E., and F. Sala. 2004. "Assessing Emotional Intelligence Competencies." *The Measurement of Emotional Intelligence*: 147–180.

Boyatzis, R. E., E. C. Stubbs, and S. N. Taylor. 2002. "Learning Cognitive and Emotional Intelligence Competencies through Graduate Management Education." *Academy of Management Journal on Learning and Education* 2: 150–162.

Brackett, M., and J. Meyer. 2003. "Convergent, Discriminant, and Incremental Validity of Competing Measures of Emotional Intelligence." *Personality and Social Psychology Bulletin* 29: 1147–58.

Brown, R., and N. Schutte. 2006. "Direct and Indirect Associations between Emotional Intelligence and Subjective Fatigue in University Students." *Journal of Psychosomatic Research* 60: 585–593.

Buelow, B. 2015. *The Introvert Entrepreneur*. New York: Penguin Random House.

Burns, L. 1994. "Gender Differences among Correlates of Career Indecision." Unpublished PhD diss., Lubbock: Texas Tech University.

Butt, T., and N. Parton. 2005. "Constructivist Social Work and Personal Construct Theory." *British Journal of Social Work* 35: 793–806.

Bye, D., D. Pushkar, and M. Conway. 2007. "Motivation, Interest, and Positive Affect in Traditional and Nontraditional Undergraduate Students." *Adult Education Quarterly* 57: 141–158.

Cain, S. 2012. *Quiet: The Power of Introverts in a World That Can't Stop Talking*. New York: Random House.

Carmeli, A. 2003. "The Association between Emotional Intelligence and Work Attitudes, Behavior and Outcomes: An Examination among Senior Managers." *Journal of Managerial Psychology* 18: 788–814.

Carmeli, A., and Z. Josman. 2006. "The Association between Emotional Intelligence, Task Performance and Organizational Citizenship Behaviors." *Human Performance* 19: 403–419.

Carnevale, A. 2000. "Community Colleges and Career Qualifications." *New Expeditions: Charting the Second Century of Community Colleges.* Issues, Paper No. 11.

Chamorro-Premuzic, T. 2019. *Why Do So Many Incompetent Men Become Leaders? (and How to Fix It).* 1st ed. Boston, MA: Harvard Business School Publishing.

Chan, D. 2007. "Leadership Competencies among Chinese Gifted Students in Hong Kong: The Connection with Emotional Intelligence and Successful Intelligence." *Roeper Review* 29, no. 3: 183–189.

Charbonneau, D., and A. Nicol. 2002. "Emotional Intelligence and Prosocial Behaviors in Adolescents." *Psychological Reports* 90: 361–370.

Chartrand, J., S. Robbins, W. Morrill, and K. Boggs. 1990. "Development and Validation of the Career Factors Inventory." *Journal of Counseling Psychology* 37: 491–501.

Chen, C. 1999. "Common Stressors among International College Students: Research and Counseling Implications." *Journal of College Counseling* 2: 49–65.

Chickering, A., and L. Reisser. 1993. *Education and Identity.* 2nd ed. San Francisco: Jossey-Bass.

Christie, A., P. Jordan, A. Troth, and S. Lawrence. 2007. "Testing the Links between Emotional Intelligence and Motivation." *Journal of Management and Organization* 13: 212–226.

Ciarrochi, J., A. Chan, and J. Bajgar. 2001. "Measuring Emotional Intelligence in Adolescents." *Personality and Individual Differences* 31: 1105–1119.

Ciarrochi, J., A. Chan, and P. Caputi. 2000. "A Critical Evaluation of the Emotional Intelligence Construct." *Personality and Individual Differences* 28: 539–561.

Clark, S., R. Callister, and R. Wallace. 2003. "Undergraduate Management Skills Courses and Students' Emotional Intelligence." *Journal of Management Education* 27: 3–24.

Clyne, C., and N. Blampied. 2004. "Training in Emotion Regulation as a Treatment for Binge Eating: A Preliminary Study." *Behavior Change* 21: 269–281.

Coleman, H. 2010. *Empowering Yourself: The Organizational Game Revealed.* 2nd ed. Bloomington, IN: AuthorHouse.

Collins, J. 2001. *Good to Great.* 1st ed. New York: HarperCollins.

Colvin, C., and J. Block. 1994. "Do Positive Illusions Foster Mental Health? An Evaluation of Taylor and Brown Formulation." *Psychological Bulletin* 116: 3–20.

Covey, S. 1989. *The 7 Habits of Highly Effective People.* 1st ed. New York: Simon & Schuster.

Creswell, J. 2008. *Educational Research: Planning, Conducting, and Evaluating Quantitative and Qualitative Research.* 3rd ed. Upper Saddle River, NJ: Pearson Education, Inc.

Daus, C. S., and N. M. Ashkanasy. 2003. "On Deconstructing the Emotional Intelligence 'Debate.'" *Industrial-Organizational Psychologist* 41: 16–18.

Davies, M., L. Stankov, and R. Roberts. 1998. "Emotional Intelligence: In Search of an Elusive Construct." *Personality Processes and Individual Differences* 75, no. 4: 989–1015.

Davis, C., and E. Asliturk. 2011. "Toward a Positive Psychology of Coping with Anticipated Events." *Canadian Psychology* 52: 101–111.

Davis, N., and M. I. Cho. 2005. "Intercultural Competence for Future Leaders of Educational Technology and Its Evaluation." *Interactive Educational Multimedia* 10: 1–22.

Davis, C., and M. Morgan. 2008. "Finding Meaning, Perceiving Growth, and Acceptance of Tinnitus." *Rehabilitation Psychology* 53: 128–138.

Day, A., and S. Carroll. 2004. "Using an Ability-Based Measure of Emotional Intelligence to Predict Individual Performance, Group Performance, and Group Citizenship Behaviors." *Personality and Individual Differences* 41: 1229–39.

Depape, A., J. Hakim-Larson, S. Voelker, S. Page, and D. Jackson. 2006. "Self-Talk and Emotional Intelligence in University Students." *Canadian Journal of Behavioural Science* 38: 250–261.

Dinh, H. 2022. "Analysis and Methods to Improve Leadership Ability for Introverts at Work." *Haaga-Helia University.*

Dipeolu, A., R. Reardon, I. Sampson, and J. Burkhcad. 2002. "The Association between Dysfunctional Career Thoughts and Adjustment to Disability in College Students with Learning Disabilities." *Journal of Career Assessment* 10: 413–427.

Druskat, V., and J. Wheeler. 2003. "Managing from the Boundary: The Effective Leadership of Self-Managing Work Teams." *Academy of Management Journal* 46: 435–57.

Druskat, V., and S. Wolff. 2001. "Building the Emotional Intelligence of Groups." *Harvard Business Review* 79: 80–90.

Duckworth, A., C. Peterson, M. Matthews, and D. Kelly. 2007. "Grit: Perseverance and Passion for Long-Term Goals." *Journal of Personal Soc. Psychol.* 92: 1087.

Dulewicz, V., and M. Higgs. 2000. "Emotional Intelligence: A Review and Evaluation Study." *Journal of Managerial Psychology* 15, no. 4: 341–372.

Earley, P. C., and S. Ang. 2003. *Cultural Intelligence: Individual Interactions across Cultures.* Palo Alto, CA: Stanford University Press.

Education Trust. 1999. "A Statement of State Education CEO's." *Thinking K–16*: 3, 10.

Elfenbein, H. A., and N. Ambady. 2003. "When Familiarity Breeds Accuracy: Cultural Exposure and Facial Emotion Recognition." *Journal of Personality and Social Psychology* 85: 276–290.

Emmerling, R., and R. Boyatzis. 2012. "Emotional and Social Intelligence Competencies: Cross-Cultural Implications." *Cross Cultural Management* 19: 4–18.

Evelyn, J. 2002. "Nontraditional Students Dominate Undergraduate Enrollments, Study Finds." *Chronicle of Higher Education* 48, no. 3: 246–263.

Fatt, J. 2002. "Emotional Intelligence: For Human Resource Managers." *Management Review News* 25: 57–74.

Faul, F., E. Erdfelder, A. Lang, and A. Buchne. 2007. "G*Power 3: A Flexible Statistical Power Analysis Program for the Social, Behavioral, and Biomedical Sciences." *Behavior Research Methods* 39: 175–191.

Ferdig, R., J. Coutts, J. DiPietro, and B. Lok. 2007. "Innovative Technologies for Multicultural Education Needs." *Multicultural Education & Technology Journal* 1: 47–63.

Forbus, P., J. Newbold, and S. Mehta, S. 2011. "A Study of Non-Traditional and Traditional Students in Terms of Their Time Management Behaviors, Stress Factors, and Coping Strategies." *Academy of Educational Leadership Journal* 15: 109–125.

Fox, F. V., and B. M. Staw. 1979. "The Trapped Administrator: Effects of Job Insecurity and Policy Resistance upon Commitment to a Course of Action." *Administrative Science Quarterly* 24: 449–472.

Gardner, H. 1993. *Multiple Intelligence: The Theory in Practice.* New York: Basic Books.

Gardner, H. 1999. *Intelligence Reframed: Multiple Intelligences for the 21ˢᵗ Century.* New York: Basic Books.

Gati, I., M. Krausz, and S. Osipow. 1996. "A Taxonomy of Difficulties in Career Decision Making." *Journal of Career Psychology* 43: 510–26.

Gelfand, M. J., L. Imai, and R. Fehr. 2008. "Thinking Intelligently about Cultural Intelligence: The Road Ahead." *Handbook on Cultural Intelligence: Theory, Measurement, and Applications*: 41–55.

Gianakos, I. 1999. "Patterns of Career Choice and Career Decision-Making Self-Efficacy." *Journal of Vocational Behavior* 54: 244–258.

Goleman, D. 1995. *Emotional Intelligence.* New York: Bantam Books.

Goleman, D. 1998. *What Makes a Leader?* Boston, MA: Harvard Business Review.

Goleman, D. 2000. "Leadership that Gets Results." *Harvard Business Review* 78: 80–90.

Goleman, D. 2006. *Social Intelligence.* New York: Bantam Dell.

Gostick, A., and C. Elton. 2007. *The Carrot Principle.* New York: Free Press.

Grant, A. 2013. "Rethinking the Extraverted Sales Ideal: The Ambivert Advantage." *Psychological Science* 24: 1024–30.

Grubb, W. 1999. "The Economic Benefits of Subbaccalaureate Education: Results from the National Studies." *Community College Research Center.*

Grubb, W., N. Badway, D. Bell, and M. Castellano. 2000. "Community Colleges Welfare Reform: Emerging Practices, Enduring Problems." *Community College Journal* 69, no. 6: 31–36.

Guastello, D., and S. Guastello. 2003. "Androgyny, Gender Role Behaviour, and Emotional Intelligence among College Students and Their Parents." *Sex Roles* 49: 663–673.

Gupta, S. 2009. *Contemporary Leadership and Intercultural Competence.* Thousand Oaks, CA: SAGE.

Haislett, J., and A. Hafer. 1990. "Predicting Success of Engineering Students during the Freshman Year." *Career Development Quarterly* 39: 86–95.

Hajj, R., and G. Dagher. 2010. "An Empirical Investigation of the Relation between Emotional Intelligence and Job Satisfaction in the Lebanese Service Industry." *Business Review, Cambridge* 16: 71–78.

Han, K., E. Yang, and S. Choi. 2001. "Research of Attitudes of College Freshmen toward Career Path." *Yonsei University Student Center Research Review* 17: 3–18.

Hannah, L., and L. Robinson. 1990. "Survey Report: How Colleges Help Freshmen Select Courses and Careers." *Journal of Career Planning and Employment* 1: 53–57.

Hartog, D. 2004. "Leading in a Global Context: Vision in Complexity." *Blackwell Handbook of Global Management.*

Hayes, R., J. Nelson, M. Tabin, G. Pearson, and C. Worthy. 2002. "Using School-Wide Data to Advocate for Student Success:

Charting the Academic Trajectory of Every Student." *Professional School Counselor* 6, no. 2: 86–94.

Heckhausen, J. 1999. *Developmental Regulation in Adulthood: Age-Normative and Sociostructural Constraints as Adaptive Challenges.* Cambridge, UK: Cambridge University Press.

Heckhausen, J., and R. Schulz. 1995. "A Life-Span Theory of Control." *Psychological Review* 102: 284–304.

Heckhausen, J., and M. Tomasik. 2002. "Get an Apprenticeship before School Is Out: How German Adolescents Adjust Vocational Aspirations When Getting Close to a Development Deadline." *Journal of Vocational Behavior* 60: 199–219.

Hochschild, A. 1983. *The Managed Heart: Commercialization of Human Feelings.* Berkeley, CA: University of California Press.

Holland, J., D. Daiger, and P. Power. 1980. *My Vocational Situation.* Palo Alto, CA: Consulting Psychologists Press.

Janis, I., and L. Mann. 1976. "Coping with Decisional Conflict: An Analysis of How Stress Affects Decision-Making Suggests Interventions to Improve the Process." *American Scientist* 64: 657–666.

Jex, S., and T. Britt. 2008. *Organizational Psychology: A Scientist-Practitioner Approach.* Hoboken, NJ: John Wiley & Sons.

Jung, C. 1921. *Psychological Types.* Princeton, NJ: Princeton University Press.

Kilk, K. 1997. "The Association between Dysfunctional Career Thought and Choosing an Academic Major." Dissertation Abstracts International.

Kim, E., and K. Oh. 1991. "A Review of Characteristics of the 1991 Yonsei University Entrants." *Yonsei University Counseling Center Research Review* 8: 3–36.

Kirkpatrick, L. 2001. "Multicultural Strategies for Community Colleges: Expanding Faculty Diversity." *ERIC Digest.*

Kolb, D. 1984. *Experiential Learning: Experience as the Source of Learning and Development.* Englewood Cliffs, NJ: Prentice-Hall.

Landy, F. J. 2003. "Emotional Intelligence: A Debate." Paper presented at the 2003 SIOP Conference, Orlando, Florida.

Larsen, J., S. Hemenover, C. Norris, and J. Cacioppo. 2003. "Turning Adversity to Advantage: On the Virtues of the Coactivation of Positive and Negative Emotions." *A Psychology of Human Strengths*. Washington, DC: American Psychological Association.

Larson, L., P. Heppner, T. Ham, and K. Dugan. 1988. "Investigating Multiple Subtypes of Career Indecision through Cluster Analysis." *Journal of Counseling Psychology* 35: 439–446.

Lasonen, J. 2003. "Interculturalisation through Music Teaching." *Lifelong Learning in Europe* 8: 10–16.

Lasonen, J. 2005. "Reflections on Interculturality in Relation to Education and Work." *Higher Education Policy* 18: 397–407.

Law, K., C. Wong, and L. Song. 2004. "The Construct and Criterion Validity of Emotional Intelligence and Its Potential Utility for Management Studies." *Journal of Applied Psychology* 89: 483–496.

Lee, K. 2005. "Coping with Career Indecision: Differences between Four Career Choice Types." *Journal of Career Development* 31: 279–89.

Lee, K., and M. C. Ashton. 2004. "Psychometric Properties of the HEXACO Personality Inventory." *Multivariate Behavioral Research* 39: 329–358.

Lee, K., and J. Han. 1997. "Validation of Measurement of Career Attitude Maturity." *Korean Journal of Career Educational Research* 8: 219–255.

Levy-Leboyer, C. 2007. "CQ: Developing Cultural Intelligence at Work." *Personnel Psychology*: 60, 242.

Liau, A. K., A. W. Liau, G. Teoh, and M. T. Liau. 2003. "The Case for Emotional Literacy: The Influence of Emotional Intelligence on Problem Behaviours in Malaysian Secondary School Students." *Journal of Moral Education* 32: 51–66.

Liff, S. 2003. "Social and Emotional Intelligence: Applications for Developmental Education." *Journal of Developmental Education* 26, no. 3: 28–32.

Likert, R. 1961. *New Patterns of Management*. New York: McGraw-Hill.

Liptak, J. 2005. "Using Emotional Intelligence to Help College Students Succeed in the Workplace." *Journal of Employment Counseling* 42: 171–178.

Locke, D. 1999. *Getting African American Male Students on Track: Working with African-American Males: A Guide to Practice.* Thousand Oaks, CA: SAGE.

Malek, T., I. Noor-Azniza, A. Muntasir, N. Mohammad, and M. Luqman. 2011. "The Effectiveness of Emotional Intelligence Training Program on Social and Academic Adjustment among First Year University Students." *International Journal of Business and Social Science* 2: 251–258.

Manz, C. C., and C. P. Neck. 1991. "Inner Leadership: Creating Productive Thought Patterns." *The Executive* 3: 71.

Markham, S. E., and I. S. Markham. 1995. "Self-Management and Self-Leadership Reexamined. A Level-of-Analysis-Perspective." *Leadership Quarterly* 6: 343–59.

Matthews, G., M. Zeidner, and R. D. Roberts. 2002. *Emotional Intelligence: Science and Myth.* Cambridge, MA: MIT Press.

Mau, W., and D. Jepsen. 1992. "Effects of Computer-Assisted Instruction in Using Formal Decision-Making Strategies to Choose a College Major." *Journal of Counseling Psychology* 39: 185–192.

Mayer, J. D. 1999. "Emotional Intelligence: Popular or Scientific Psychology?" *APA Monitor* 30: 50.

Mayer, J. D., and C. D. Cobb. 2000. "Educational Policy on Emotional Intelligence: Does It Make Sense?" *Educational Psychology Review* 12: 163–183.

Mayer, J., and P. Salovey. 1997. "What Is Emotional Intelligence?" In *Emotional Development and Emotional Intelligence: Implications for Educators*, edited by P. Salovey and D. Sluyter, 3–34. New York: Basic Books.

Mayer, J., P. Salovey, and D. Caruso. 2000. "Competing Models of Emotional Intelligence." *Handbook of Intelligence*, 396–420.

McEnrue, M. P., K. S. Groves, and W. Shen. 2009. "Emotional Intelligence Development: Leveraging Individual Characteristics." *Journal of Management Development* 28: 150–174.

McGregor, D. 1960. *The Human Side of Enterprise.* New York: McGraw-Hill.

Mentkowski, M. 2000. *Learning That Lasts: Integrating Learning, Development, and Performance in College and Beyond.* San Francisco: Jossey-Bass.

Meyer, B., and J. Winer. 1993. "The Career Decision Scale and Neuroticism." *Journal of Career Assessment* 1: 171–180.

Momeni, N. 2009. "The Association between Managers' Emotional Intelligence and the Organizational Climate They Create." *Public Personnel Management* 38: 35–48.

Moore, J. W., B. Jensen, and W. Hauck. 1990. "Decision-Making Processes of Youth." *Adolescence* 25: 583–592.

Morris, E., P. Brooks, and J. May. 2003. "The Relationship between Achievement Goal Orientation and Coping Style." *College Student Journal* 37: 3–8.

Neimeyer, R., and S. Baldwin. 2003. "Personal Construct Psychotherapy and the Constructivist Horizon." In *International Handbook of Personal Construct Psychology.* Chichester: Wiley.

Nelson, D., and G. Low. 2003. *Emotional Intelligence: Achieving Academic and Career Excellence.* Upper Saddle River, NJ: Prentice Hall.

Newbold, J., S. Mehta, and Forbus. 2010. "A Comparative Study between Non-Traditional Students in Terms of Their Demographics, Attitudes, Behavior and Educational Performance." *International Journal of Education Research* 5, no. 1: 1–24.

Newcombe, M., and N. Ashkanasy. 2002. "The Role of Affect and Affective Congruence in Perceptions of Leaders: An Experimental Study." *Leadership Quarterly* 13: 601–614.

Ng, K., C. Wang, C. Zalaquett, and N. Bodehorn. 2007. "A Confirmatory Factor Analysis of the Wong and Law Emotional

Intelligence Scale in a Sample of International College Students."
International Journal for the Advancement of Counseling 29: 173–185.

Ng, K. Y., and C. P. Earley. 2006. "Culture + Intelligence: Old Constructs, New Frontiers." *Group & Organization Management* 31: 4–19.

Ngunjiri, F., L. Schumacher, and K. Bowman. 2009. "Global Business Leadership: The Need for Emotional and Cultural Intelligence." Paper presented at the International Leadership Association Conference, November 12–15, 2009.

Niederhoffer, K., and J. Pennebaker. 2009. "Sharing One's Story: On the Benefits of Writing or Talking about Emotional Experience." In *Handbook of Positive Psychology*, edited by S. J. Lopez and C. R. Snyder. New York: Oxford University Press.

Oelwang, J. 2022. "Partnering: Forge the Deep Connections That Make Great Things Happen." New York: Optimism Press.

Oginska-Bulik, N. 2005. "Emotional Intelligence in the Workplace: Exploring Its Effects on Occupational Stress and Health Outcomes in Human Service Workers." *International Journal of Occupational Medicine and Environmental Health* 18: 167–175.

Okpala, C., L. Hopson, and A. Okpala. 2011. "The Impact of Current Economic Crisis on Community Colleges." *College Student Journal* 45: 214–216.

Olson, S. 2009. "Craving for Convenience Fuels Ivy Tech Online Boom." *Indianapolis Business Journal* 29: 18–19.

Osipow, S. 1987. *The Career Decision Scale Manual.* Odessa, FL: Psychological Assessment Resources.

Osipow, S., and J. Winer. 1996. "The Use of the Career Decision Scale in Career Assessment." *Journal of Career Assessment* 4: 117–130.

Paige, R. M. 2004. "The Intercultural in Teaching and Learning: A Developmental Perspective." Paper presented at University of South Australia, Adelaide, 1–15.

Painter, C. 2004. "The Association between Adults Reporting Symptoms of Attention Deficit Hyperactivity Disorder and

Dysfunctional Career Beliefs and Job Satisfaction." Dissertation Abstracts International.

Palmer, B., G. Gignac, R. Manocha, and C. Stough. 2005. "A Psychometric Evaluation of the Mayer-Salovey-Caruso Emotional Intelligence Test Version 2.0." *Intelligence* 33: 285–305.

Pascarella, E. T., and P. T. Terenzini. 1991. *How College Affects Students: Findings and Insights from Twenty Years of Research.* San Francisco: Jossey-Bass.

Pau, A., and R. Croucher. 2003. "Emotional Intelligence and Perceived Stress in Dental Undergraduates." *Journal of Dental Education* 67: 1023–1028.

Pedersen, P. 1991. "Counseling International Students." *Counseling Psychologist* 19: 10–58.

Peters, N. 2010. "Baby Boomers Attending a Community College: Influences, Challenges, and Social Networks." PhD diss. Retrieved from ProQuest.

Peterson, G., J. Sampson, J. Lenz, and R. Reardon. 2002. "A Cognitive Information Processing Approach in Career Problem Solving and Decision Making." *Career Choice and Development.* 4th ed. San Francisco: Jossey-Bass.

Petrides, K., and A. Furnham. 2006. "Trait EI in Workplace." *Journal of Applied Social Psychology* 36 (2): 552–569.

Phelam, D. 2000. "Enrollment Policy and Student Access at Community Colleges. A Policy Paper." *Education Commission of the States, Center for Community College Policy.*

Polychroniou, P. 2009. "Association between Emotional Intelligence and Transformational Leadership of Supervisors: The Impact on Team Effectiveness." *Team Performance Management* 15: 343–58.

Popoola, T., and Karadas, G. 2022. "How Impactful are Grit, I-deals, and the Glass Ceiling on Subjective Career Success?" *Sustainability*: 1136.

Porter, L., and L. McKibbin. 1988. *Management Education and Development: Drift or Thrust into the 21st Century?* New York: McGraw-Hill.

Poyrazli, S., C. Arbona, R. Bullington, and S. Pisecco. 2001. "Adjustment Issues of Turkish College Students Studying in the United States." *College Student Journal* 35: 52–62.

Quale, A., and A. Schanke. 2010. "Resilience in the Face of Coping with a Severe Physical Injury: A Study of Trajectories of Adjustment in a Rehabilitation Setting." *Rehabilitation Psychology* 55: 12–22.

Ramsey, R. 2021. *Show Me the Money.* Bloomington, IN: AuthorHouse.

Reker, G., and P. Wong. 1988. "Aging as an Individual Process: Toward a Theory of Personal Meaning." *Handbook of Theories of Aging.* New York: Springer.

Riley, H., and N. Schutte. 2003. "Low Emotional Intelligence as a Predictor of Substance-Use Problems." *Journal of Drug Education* 33: 391–398.

Roberts, R., M. Zeidner, and G. Matthews. 2001. "Does Emotional Intelligence Meet Traditional Standards for an Intelligence? Some New Data and Conclusions." *Emotions* 1: 196–231.

Saklofske, D., E. Austin, J. Galloway, and K. Davidson. 2007. "Individual Difference Correlates of Health-Related Behaviours: Preliminary Evidence for Links between Emotional Intelligence and Coping." *Personality and Individual Differences* 42: 491–502.

Saklofske, D., E. Austin, and P. Minski. 2003. "Factor Structure and Validity of a Trait Emotional Intelligence Measure." *Personality and Individual Differences* 34: 1091–1100.

Salovey, P., and J. D. Mayer. 1990. "Emotional Intelligence." *Imagination, Cognition, and Personality* 9: 185–211.

Saunders, D., J. Sampson, G. Peterson, and R. Reardon. 2000. "Relation of Depression and Dysfunctional Career Thinking to Career Indecision." *Journal of Vocational Behavior* 56: 288–298.

Schumacher, L., J. Wheeler, and A. Carr. 2009. "The Association between Emotional Intelligence and Buyer's Performance." *Journal of Business & Industrial Marketing* 24: 269–277.

Schutte, N., and J. Malouff. 1998. "Developmental and Interpersonal Aspects of Emotional Intelligence." Paper presented at the Convention of the American Psychological Society, Washington, DC.

Schutte, N., and J. Malouff. 2002. "Incorporating Emotional Skills in a College Transition Course Enhances Student Retention." *Journal of the First-Year Experience and Students in Transition* 14: 7–21.

Schutte, N., J. Malouff, and N. Bhullar. 2009. "The Assessing Emotions Scale." In *The Assessment of Emotional Intelligence*, edited by C. Stough, D. Sakofske, and J. Parker. New York: Springer Publishing.

Schutte, N., J. Malouff, C. Bobik, T. Conston, C. Greeson, C. Jedlicka, E. Rhodes, and G. Wendorf. 2001. "Emotional Intelligence and Interpersonal Relations." *Journal of Social Psychology* 141: 523–536.

Schutte, N., J. Malouff, L. Hall, D. Haggerty, J. Cooper, C. Golden. 1998. "Development and Validation of a Measure of Emotional Intelligence." *Personality and Individual Differences* 25: 167–177.

Schutte, N., J. Malouff, M. Simunek, J. McKenley, and S. Hollander. 2002. "Characteristic Emotional Intelligence and Emotional Well-Being." *Cognition and Emotion* 16: 769–786.

Scott, G., J. Ciarrochi, and F. Deane. 2004. "Disadvantages of Being an Individualist in an Individualistic Culture: Idiocentrism, Emotional Competence, Stress, and Mental Health." *Australian Psychologist* 39: 143–153.

Seligman, M., and M. Csikzszentmihalyi. 2000. "Positive Psychology: An Introduction." *American Psychologist* 55: 5–14.

Sewell, K. 2003. "An Approach to Posttraumatic Stress." *International Handbook of Personal Construct Psychology*. Chichester: Wiley.

Shipley, N., M. Jackson, and S. Segrest. 2010. "The Effects of Emotional Intelligence, Age, Work Experience, and Academic Performance." *Research in Higher Education Journal* 9: 1–18.

Shivpuri, S., and B. Kim. 2004. "Do Employers and Colleges See Eye-to-Eye? College Student Development and Assessment." *NACE Journal* 65: 37–44.

Sjoberg, L. 2001. "Emotional Intelligence: A Psychometric Analysis." *European Psychologist* 6: 79–95.

Staw, B. 1976. "Knee-Deep in the Big Muddy: The Effect of Personal Responsibility and Decision Consequences upon Commitment to a Previously Chosen Course of Action." *Organizational Behavior and Human Performance* 16: 27–44.

Sternberg, R. J. 2002. "Foreword." In *Emotional Intelligence: Science and Myth*, edited by G. Matthews, A. Zeidner, and R. Roberts, xi–xiii. Cambridge, MA: The MIT Press.

Taylor, S., and J. Brown. 1988. "Illusions and Well-Being: A Social Psychological Perspective on Mental Health." *Psychological Bulletin* 103: 193–210.

Thingujam, N., and U. Ram. 2000. "Emotional Intelligence Scale: Indian Norms." *Journal of Education and Psychology* 58: 40–48.

Thorndike, R., and S. Stein. 1937. "An Evaluation of the Attempts to Measure Social Intelligence." *Psychological Bulletin* 34: 275–284.

Totterdell, P., and D. Holman. 2003. "Emotion Regulation in Customer Service Roles: Testing a Model of Emotional Labor." *Journal of Occupational Health Psychology* 8: 55–73.

Tucker, M., J. Sojka, F. Barone, and A. McCarthy. 2000. "Training Tomorrow's Leaders: Enhancing the Emotional Intelligence of Business Graduates." *Journal of Education for Business* 75: 331–37.

US Department of Education, Office of Educational Research and Improvement, National Center for Education Statistics. 1999. "The Condition of Education." http://www.nces.ed.gov/pubs2001/2001022.pdf.

Van Rooy, D., A. Alonso, and C. Viswesvaran. 2005. "Group Differences in Emotional Intelligence Scores: Theoretical and Practical Implications." *Personality and Individual Differences* 38: 689–700.

Vayrynen, R. 1997. *Global Transformation: Economics, Politics, and Culture*. Helsinki: Gaudeamus.

Webb, K. 2009. "Why Emotional Intelligence Should Matter to Management: A Survey of the Literature." *S.A.M. Advanced Management Journal* 74: 32–43.

Wechsler, D. 1943. "Nonintellective Factors in General Intelligence." *Psychological Bulletin* 37: 444–445.

Wechsler, D. 1958. *The Measurement and Appraisal of Adult Intelligence*. 4th ed. Baltimore, MD: The Williams and Wilkins Company.

Williams, J., and M. Luo. 2010. "Understanding First-Year Persistence at a Micropolitan University: Do Geographic Characteristics of Students' Home City Matter?" *College Student Journal* 44: 362–376.

Wing, J., N. Schutte, and B. Byrne. 2006. "The Effect of Positive Writing on Emotional Intelligence and Life Satisfaction." *Journal of Clinical Psychology* 62: 1291–1302.

Winter, D. G., D. C. McClellend, and A. J. Stewart. 1981. *A New Case for the Liberal Arts: Assessing Institutional Goals and Student Development*. San Francisco: Jossey-Bass.

Wong, C. S., and K. S. Law. 2002. "The Effects of Leader and Follower Emotional Intelligence on Performance and Attitude: An Exploratory Study." *Leadership Quarterly* 13: 243–274.

Wrosch, C., and J. Heckhausen. 1999. "Control Processes before and after Passing a Developmental Deadline: Activation and Deactivation of Intimate Association Goals." *Journal of Personality and Social Psychology* 77: 415–427.

Xanthopoulou, D., A. Bakker, E. Demerouti, and W. Schaufeli. 2009. "Work Engagement and Financial Returns: A Diary Study of the Role of Job and Personal Resources." *Journal of Occupational and Organizational Psychology* 82: 183–200.

Yanchak, K., S. Lease, and D. Strauser. 2005. "Relation of Disability Type and Career Thoughts to Vocational Identity." *Rehabilitation Counseling Bulletin* 48: 130–138.

Yarrish, K., and M. Law. 2009. "An Exploration on the Differences in Emotional Intelligence of First Year Students Examined across Disciplines within the School of Business in a Liberal Arts College." *Contemporary Issues in Education Research* 2: 47–53.

Yurtsever, G. 2003. "Measuring the Moral Entrepreneurial Personality." *Social Behavior and Personality* 31: 1–12.

Yuvaraj, S., and N. Srivastava. 2007. "Are Innovative Managers Emotionally Intelligent?" *Journal of Management Research* 7: 169–178.

Zeiss, T. 2006. "Baby Boomers: An Encore Opportunity." *Community College Journal*: 39–41.

Zizzi, S., H. Deaner, and D. Hirschhorn. 2003. "The Association between Emotional Intelligence and Performance among College Baseball Players." *Journal of Applied Sport Psychology* 15: 262–269.

Printed in the United States
by Baker & Taylor Publisher Services